D1336465

Old
Japan

Oh country which has become so dear to me, is this progress really progress, this civilisation really civilisation for you? I, who have admired the artlessness of your inhabitants as well as their simple customs, who has seen the abundance of your fertile fields, who has heard everywhere the happy laughter of your children, and have never been able to discern misery, oh, I fear God, that this scene of happiness is coming to an end and that the Occidental people [Westerners] will bring here their fatal vices.

Journal of Henry Heusken, 7 December 1857

Old Japan

SECRETS FROM THE SHORES OF THE SAMURAI

ANTONY CUMMINS

The History Press

First published 2018

The History Press
The Mill, Brimscombe Port
Stroud, Gloucestershire, GL5 2QG
www.thehistorypress.co.uk

British Library Cataloguing in Publication Data.
A catalogue record for this book is available from the British Library.

ISBN 978 0 7509 8442 3

Typesetting and origination by The History Press
Printed and bound in Great Britain by TJ International Ltd

Contents

Foreword by
Lord Redesdale

My great-grandfather, A.B. Mitford, 1st Lord Redesdale, was everything a dashing Victorian was meant to be: adventurous, a scholar and extremely brave. However, where he differed from many was that he really tried not only to understand but, in a time of fast-moving change, record the culture of the Japan of the 1860s – from the age of the shogun, which tried to prevent foreign influence, to a society that embraced progress, at a rate that led to the loss of many traditions that he experienced first-hand. Most travellers, after a brief stay in a country, believe they have a clear understanding of how that country works. This is probably due to the veneer of globalisation that affects almost all countries these days. However, from Mitford's writings it is clear that only when he had finished his tour of duty at the Embassy and looked back many years later did he realise that his deep knowledge had left him with far more questions than he had in the first place.

Mitford recorded many customs, practices and folk tales he came across while in Japan; however, most of his writings were published much later in life. His writing may have been influenced through looking back, but the image it evoked is of a culture he loved. His gift as a writer led to the books becoming very popular and, it can be suggested, would have been one of many reasons that there was so much interest in Japanese art and culture.

We tend to forget, being able to travel to Japan in a day, how inaccessible the country was in the nineteenth century. It is hardly surprising that the Victorians would have had little knowledge about the country, and his descriptions would have given a rare insight. Mitford's recollections would have been one of the few sources available. It is ironic that, for most, their idea of life in Japan was the picture created by the comic opera *The Mikado*. It is fitting therefore that there is evidence Mitford was consulted on costumes to ensure their authenticity for the opera. I have in the library a book incorporating all the flyers, pictures and descriptions of the many amateur dramatic productions Mitford took part in throughout his life, giving context to his link with Gilbert and Sullivan. The comic opera was the second longest-running musical at the time, showing how the exotic theme touched a chord with London society.

Mitford's life changed after he returned from Japan: he inherited an estate in Gloucestershire and land in Redesdale, Northumberland, from his cousin. His cousin's title of earl, however, was not passed to him. Family legend has it that, as a drinking companion of the Prince Regent, Queen Victoria blocked him from taking the title. There may be some truth in this as he was created Lord Redesdale two years after she died. It was as Lord Redesdale that he took part in the Garter mission to Japan, seeing a country that had shifted fundamentally as a culture.

Having read many of Mitford's accounts, I have always wanted to visit Japan and managed my first trip earlier this year. Japan is a fascinating place that has adopted the trappings of globalised culture in a uniquely Japanese blend. Like Mitford, I am sure I could spend years immersed in Japan without really understanding such a complex and multi-layered society. The one thing that has not changed is the warmth of the welcome. I am sure that even though the changes would make modern Japan totally alien to Mitford, if he were to visit today, unlike many cultures, he would see how much of the culture has survived rather than how much has been lost.

Lord Redesdale
February 2018

Introduction

The Magic
of Old Japan

Flavour Not Ingredients

If history were a cake, the individual contests between historians would be the ingredients, the complex parts that make up the whole 'meal' of history, while the myths, legends, stories, anecdotes and traditions would be the 'flavour'. There are plenty of volumes out there with competitive arguments, debates, analysis and historiography, but this book is not one of them. This book is the smell of a scone from a wood-lit stove, it is the waft of bacon in the morning and the aroma of port and cheese – it is the flavour of the story of Japan.

The historical basis for this book are the numerous records of European travellers who have been visiting Japan since the 1500s – those men and women who travelled the gruelling seas and passed entire continents by way of tall ship to arrive in the famed land of the barbarian knights with their savage scimitars. These special accounts are stored in uniformed rows of books in university libraries, packed away in college journals or found in now long out of print diaries. They range from Jesuit accounts of the 1500s, to ships' logs and seamen's diaries, to diplomats' journals and travellers' letters, all of them the thoughts, statements and recordings of those people who saw the samurai for real and who witnessed such times with their own eyes. From these accounts I have taken the mysterious, the interesting, the exciting and the curious and laid them out here for readers to enjoy in a bite-sized manner. Each chapter holds an array of small sections which in turn hold the essence of the above accounts, removing the laborious but highlighting those parts that are worth remembering. In addition to this are extracts and assimilations from various academic journals and books that hold key and fascinating ideas about Japan but which are locked between long and complex arguments. It is there, inside that space where the interesting is encased in the stonework of historical debate, that I have searched out the best elements and brought them together to form the essence of Japan – a touch of warm nostalgia of days long gone. I want this aroma of old ways to waft over the world as copies of this book reach its far corners, and I wish to spread the experience of a lost world, the accounts and tales to be shared and passed on, generation after generation. Japan, being a most ancient and traditional land, has deep enriched soil filled with the memories of linked generations. The echo of their stories continues down the ages and is brought to the modern world, through these bygone travellers in Japan, and is laid out for you here to relish and enjoy.

Travellers in Japan

Japan is always considered to have been a 'closed country' but this was actually a relatively later affair in its history. Before the 1600s, Japan was very much open to trade and influence from others, even having a large Christian community. Many Western travellers came to Japan, all of whom have a great story to tell and in some cases witnessed a great deal of samurai ways and found themselves in Japan in the most exciting times. Examples of these are Francis Xavier, a Jesuit missionary who landed in Japan in 1549 at the height of the warring periods and who wrote fascinating accounts of his times there, and João Rodrigues in the late 1500s, another missionary who wrote extensively on Japanese ways and retired to Macao in the 1600s. Luís Fróis, who arrived in Japan in 1563 as a missionary, wrote many letters and histories; he died in 1597 while still in the country. Not only missionaries but also sailors such as Richard Cocks, an Englishman who stayed in Japan for trade, who wrote an extensive diary on life in Japan and died on the way back to England in 1624. The famous William Adams, the first Englishman to arrive in Japan in 1600, became a samurai and close retainer of the shogun, married a Japanese woman and became the lord of a small area (the novel *Shogun* by James Clavell is loosely based on his life, and was the inspiration for the television series *Shogun*). Of course, when the country closed its borders, the number of visitors decreased and then accounts began again in the 1800s when Japan started to open, or at least think about opening, for trade. Diplomats such as Sir Harry Parkes and Townsend Harris began to involve themselves with the Japanese government and the samurai. This even included the sad tale of Henricus (Henry) Heusken, a diplomat and assistant to Townsend Harris, who was assassinated in 1861 at the age of 28. Finally, Lord Algernon Bertram

Mitford – second secretary to the British Legation working in Japan from the 1860s – recorded and published much information on Japanese culture and history, presented the Japanese Emperor with the Order of the Garter, was a prominent figure in the changing landscape and was instrumental in bringing Japan to the modern era. He will be mentioned in this book simply as Mitford. All of these people had great stories to tell and, with a small amount of 'digging', some fascinating facts about Japanese ways and culture come to the surface, and through these eyewitnesses we see Japan fill with colour.

Historical Accuracy and Contradiction

The sections in this book are mainly taken from European eyewitnesses and their records of Japan, but also from a select few academic researchers on Japanese culture, economics, social history and the like, meaning that the foundations for all these stories are solid, no matter how light-heartedly they have been presented. However, the basic premise of history is for historians to counter each other, digging into theory and facts until a truth becomes evident. There is no room or place in this book for long debate on the accuracy of these eyewitness accounts. Therefore, when selecting them I have chosen the ones that appear to have the best claim as accurate examples of Japan itself. For example, many of these witnesses spoke about the Japanese Emperor, but often contradict or directly copy each other. In truth, many of them had never actually seen the Emperor of Japan, while some of them had. To deal with this I either dropped such articles or formed the grammar around them to show a slight wariness of the account, displaying to you that this may or may not be true but it is what was believed to be so. Sometimes I openly point out that a statement may be dubious. I have also avoided overusing the terms 'it is said', 'it was recorded', 'one account says', etc. They are inserted into a few examples to remind you that these are mainly accounts from travellers, but it would be cumbersome to maintain it for each section. In addition to this, there do appear to be many contradictions, such as punishments, the power of women, rules in society, beliefs, etc. However, these accounts are taken from all over Japan, from tip to toe, and span 1,000 years of change. Therefore, contradictions are mainly a result of differences from province to province and from century to century. At one point, the freedom of women is extensive and at others they are virtual prisoners; in another place, the life of peasants may be free and easy at one time and at others oppressed. Remember, 1,000 years is a long time and for some of that time Japan was divided, giving a constant flux of rules, regulations, customs and social situations. Start each story in your mind with 'once upon a time in Japan' and you will not go wrong.

The Boring Stuff

The purpose of this book is to simplify and make accessible the 'flavour' of Japan, not the details. Therefore, while it is based on eyewitness accounts, historical research, articles, journals and all the other lovely words that carry weight, such as footnotes, endnotes, appendices and the like, it needs those parts stripped away so that you can 'feast' on Japanese culture. My task is to read academic and sluggish material, to digest it and to bring it to you, the reader, in a way that you can enjoy, a way that allows you to ingest it in small bites. Therefore, I have added no footnotes to this book, there are no references, Japanese words are kept to an absolute minimum – apart from where they are needed to understand the story or point – and I have removed all macrons from vowels, so Tōkyō becomes Tokyo. Equally, where possible I have avoided using the word 'century' and have changed sixteenth century to 1500s, so there is no need to pause and recalculate, the only exception being the twentieth century. Furthermore, I have tried to mix up the subjects as much as possible within each chapter, making it something you can dip in and out of any time you like without having to remember where you were, or what came before. Any points that do build on each other have been kept together but each one can still stand alone. Therefore, read this book during a tea break, place it on a bathroom shelf, dip into it to tell your children short stories about the strange land in the

East, or read sections out at a dinner party – it is for these reasons have laid the book out in this manner. For those people who want those rigorous details, the bibliography is at the back of the book and details can be found through them.

Let's Get Ready to Rumble

With all of the above understood, get ready to engage with the anecdotes and yarns from across Japan's history, to be awash with its secrets, its blood-soaked memories, its brightness and its moods. Trudge in its dark times and yomp across its spring hills, frolic in its summer stories and wade through its winter tales, but above all enjoy Japan and spread her beauty and culture to the rest of the world.

Antony Cummins
2018

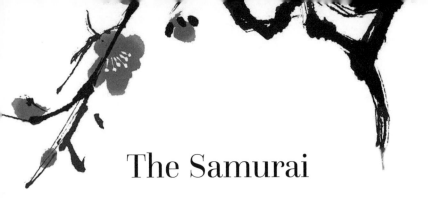

The Samurai

The Way of the Warrior

Everybody has heard of *bushido* – the way of the warrior – but many people think of it as a modern invention because a man called Nitobe Inazo wrote the book *Bushido* in English in 1900 in response to questions about society in Japan. However, that is simply not true. While the details of this chivalric code may have changed over time, the concept of *bushido* dates back many hundreds of years and is sometimes referred to simply as *budo*, a word that today has come to mean martial arts. The earliest record I have personally found for the term *bushido* is in a *c.*1495 collection of poetry by Monk Sogi. The ideograms for *bushido* are 武士道 but, when written down in poem form, the word *bushi*, meaning warrior, changes its pronunciation to *mononofu* and *do* changes to *michi*, so that the correct amount of syllables are used in the poem. This means that while the ideograms and meaning are the same, the reading changes from *bushido* to *mononofu no michi*.

The *c.*1495 poem goes thus:

Hakanaki mono wa,
Mononofu no michi
Ta ga tame no
Na nareba mi yori
Oshimran

A thing of uncertainty
Is the way of the warrior
For whose glory does a man care
less for life
Than for honour

The Etiquette of Swords

A samurai had to take his *katana* off his waist when he entered a house and hold it in hand. It was then placed in the correct storage space. At times he also kept it at his side.

The Samurai at Dinner

A retainer was a samurai who served another (normally samurai) master. They formed a bond of master–retainer in which the lower person served with obedience, forming a gap between them at societal level. However, when dining together, the conversation was free; the retainer might talk to whomever he wished and be familiar and merry. When the meal was over, his attitude returned to one of service and the gap was established again.

The Golden Age of Barrierless Society

At the start of the rise of the samurai, between the 1100s and the 1400s, the family a samurai was born into was extremely important. By the mid 1500s, almost anyone could rise to be a great lord, and even merchants became great samurai lords, making this era the greatest time for anyone with ambition. However, even at this point people had to make up false geneographies to 'prove' they were of samurai origin and, not only that, but that they descended from an imperial line by being a part of the great samurai foundation families.

Men in Armour

Films and the media often portray the samurai without their armour in the period of peace – the last 250 years of their rule – and in film after film the samurai walk around in the plain clothes of the day. However, even in the last era of the samurai the warriors of Japan still donned their armour for parades, ceremonies, when performing certain duties and in other situations. Even though the samurai were at relative peace for generations, their armour was still a major factor and they would have been used to wearing it – if, of course, they owned it.

Where Did the Guns Go?

The general public will say that the soul of a samurai is his sword, but the more enlightened reader will know that gun production was massive in Japan during the second half of the 1500s and that guns played a large role in the unification of the country – a role that cannot be ignored and a move that changed the face of samurai warfare. In 1600 the country entered into relative peace (it was actually a dictatorship, to be fair) and it is then that we get the age of the samurai with two swords at his side, so the question that springs up is, as Japan was a massive producer of guns, where are they all? Well, they became very restricted and their power had been proven, so the country returned to its glory ideas of the samurai with older weapons, such as the bow and the spear.

Around the time of the fifth shogun – also known as the dog shogun – the gun became an item reserved for the powerful, and strict control was used to stop uprisings. In the 1500s and early 1600s, Japanese guns were of similar quality to Western versions, but because of the closing of Japan, and only a small amount of trade being allowed, and with the restriction on guns, the development of firearms did not match that in the West, so, of course, when the West returned, over 200 years later, the difference was manifest.

Kill Me if You Can

One later account of samurai vengeance states that if a brother or the like was killed, a samurai had to kill the killer in revenge. The samurai would then take the head of their family member's assassin and place it on the grave of the victim, but they would leave their personal mark such as a small knife (possibly a *kozuka*) which they stuck through the ear of the severed head, meaning that any family member of the samurai who had just been killed would know how to follow up on the next stage of revenge – and so forming lasting blood feuds.

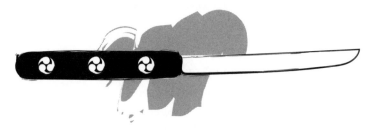

Categorising Allies

There were some basic terms used in the samurai world to categorise those who were allies:

Kamon – family members and relatives
Fudai – families who had served for many generations
Tozama – families outside of direct control.

After 1600 and the Battle of Sekigahara, these terms took on additional meanings. As the country was in the power of the Tokugawa family, almost all clans became generational retainers, so this division came to be known as those who did or did not serve the Tokugawa family in their rise to power, meaning that some samurai were born on the wrong side of a war that was long over and over which they had no control.

The Samurai Blood Oath

When a samurai said they would follow a master or they gave a promise, they often used a blood oath, which involved a cut to the finger or other places on the body, depending on the situation, and writing a vow. However, one version of the blood oath was extremely interesting:

> Make the vow in speech
> Cut the arm or hand
> Write the vow on paper in blood
> Burn the paper
> Mix the ash with liquid and drink it

Samurai on the March

Early in samurai times they would march out to war and search the countryside for rations, despoiling the land as the army moved past. This caused massive issues for locals, as often food was either taken or paid for but still used up. To counter this, new war taxes were established to feed an army on the march.

The Truth of Samurai Honour

One of my main objectives is to bring about a more realistic understanding of Japanese and samurai honour. The version the world understands is the version of pre- and post-Second World War. The twentieth century saw the samurai image being used in Japan and the rest of the world to promote the idea of a form of fairy-tale honour system. The glamourous and chivalric knight who never retreats, never surrenders and always fights. It is not my intent to mislabel the samurai or to veer into negativity, but they must be viewed through the eyes of historical truth.

Retreat: samurai did retreat; they had complex tactics on the subject.

Flee: the samurai did break and flee; many defeated samurai fled and formed villages in distant places and some even fled to South East Asia.

Suicide: some samurai would commit suicide at the death of the lord, as a voluntary custom, but many did not.

Oaths: oaths were given and a samurai's word was strong, but history is full of samurai who broke their word and changed sides, performed political murders and plainly went against their vows.

Justice: samurai did attempt to keep the peace of the land, but it was not long before many of them wanted more power and war erupted again.

Corruption: unfortunately, corruption goes hand in hand with power, and corruption can be found in samurai ways.

Honour: a samurai was focused on honour but what we consider as honourable may not have been so to them. Honour is an ethical code and all ethical codes change with time.

Consider this. When the Tokugawa Clan took over all of Japan, they had the obedience of the entire population and all families were subject to the shogun and owed him loyalty. But the shogun did not trust this 'loyalty' – rightly so, because most did not want to give it but were forced to by their defeat at the Battle of Sekigahara. Therefore, to ensure loyalty a hostage system was developed. Each great house had to put their close relatives and heir apparent in a palace in the capital city, and the warlords had to spend one year at home and one year in the capital. This meant that 'loyalty' was ensured but not given. Even with an oath, samurai loyalty was often not so strong when it came to power and climbing the hierarchical ladder.

Loyalty, Loss and Honour

The subject of male bands bounded by loyalty is a complex one, and while there is no doubt that samurai did maintain honour, it must be realised that honour systems are also bound up with fear and loss. There is fear of retribution for lack of loyalty, and fear of the loss of lands and income. While the samurai did value honour, these two elements must be taken into account; often the samurai were looking out for themselves and trying to climb the social ladder.

The Three Roles of the Samurai

We often imagine the samurai to be only warriors, but this is not quite the case. While all of them are considered warriors, there are actually three broad categories that they fall into:

 State administrators or public and private officials

 Agricultural overseers, local gentry and landowners

 Masters of war

East Side and West Side

The USA has East v. West, the UK has North v. South, and likewise old Japan had its own version. The lineage for the Japanese Emperor is divided into Northern and Southern Dynasties, with some people still offering contention on this point 700 years after the fact. The samurai themselves used to divide between Eastern samurai and Western samurai. Here is an extract from a samurai from the east side who is talking about the difference between the two, and he is very biased about the 'facts':

Warriors of the East Side
Eastern landowning gentry have 500 mounted warriors each at their command
Mounted warriors of the east never fall from their horses
If the father or son of an eastern warrior falls, that warrior will ride over his corpse to get to the enemy

Warriors of the Western Side
If the father or son of a western warrior is killed, he will leave the battlefield and cry
If a western samurai army run out of food, they halt the war and return to plant more crops
In summer they are too hot and in winter they are too cold; they are soft indeed

The Problem with Inheritance

Feudal society has an extremely problematic and fundamental issue at its core, which is inheritance. Originally, samurai used to divide their land between all their children equally, splitting up the land and property. However, the power of the samurai was based on crop production, crop production is based on land ownership, and there is a certain amount needed to maintain life as a samurai: the land needed to produce enough profit to pay for armour, horses, weapons, servants, entertainment and all the other facets of court and a privileged life. However, mathematics defeated the samurai – as the population increased more samurai were created. If a father had four sons surviving him, then the land needed to support four new samurai. If they all had four sons who survived them, the same land now had to provide for sixteen samurai. Therefore the samurai were bent on invasion and land grabbing; without it, they could not exist. To counter this, the inheritance system changed and the eldest son took total control of the land and the position of retainer to the lord, and the 'lesser' sons took a livelihood from the land on a much smaller scale. This system allowed a clan to maintain its size and importance without dividing it up into too many branches. But, again, mathematics won out and the point came when there was just not enough land. Samurai would sell what land they had to produce cash flow to maintain a samurai lifestyle; they would pawn items and even take on jobs, manufacture small items or marry into rich merchant families, all to try to maintain the samurai lifestyle. Unfortunately, this story does not have a happy ending, as by the end of the samurai era, the average samurai was relatively poor in society, and many modern Japanese films are based on this idea of the declining and threadbare samurai trying to make ends meet in life. By the 1860s, the ways of the samurai were coming to an end and, while many powerful samurai clans still held large quantities of land, most samurai lived in castle towns on an ever-dwindling wage which just could not support them.

The Breakdown of the Clan

The move to make the eldest son the sole heir and the rest of the family dependants led to intra-family strife. Each family would split off into multiple branches and a complex clan system developed. The automatic inheritance by the oldest caused problems and this at times led to inter-branch warfare within the clan and massive family disputes.

Six Generations Away

In samurai history there were four great clans that formed the basis of the roots of 'proper samurai', and not to be connected to one of these four could be be seen as a social stain. Two of these were the Taira and the Minamoto clans. The reason they were considered proper is that they were members of the imperial family. In the early days of samurai times, the imperial family was becoming too large and too difficult to support and so they announced a six-generation cut-off point. Anyone who came after that point was 'transferred' into one of these powerful families. This meant that all samurai wanted to be connected to one of these families because it meant they had a connection to the imperial line.

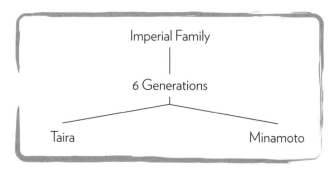

Imperial Family

6 Generations

Taira   Minamoto

The Right to Kill

It is often said that the samurai had the right to kill the peasants below them, which is legally correct; however, it was not a case of wanton violence. By the mid 1700s the samurai class had disarmed the peasants and taken almost sole control of military weapons, setting up a legal system that restricted uprisings, including rights to kill lower-class people. However, this should not be seen as a common occurrence. A samurai still had to behave well and maintain proper respect. Simply walking around killing people was not a realistic way to maintain society if you did not want constant uprisings. Therefore, the threat was there and would have been carried out in some situations. However, in the main, samurai did not walk around randomly killing people who did not bow. In fact, in the capital cities they often rubbed shoulders with each other.

Use a Middleman

The Japanese often used a middleman and go-between to do business. It has been theorised that this was to stop fights and arguments. Remembering that among the samurai a fight involved swords, vendetta and most likely blood and death, the use of a middleman stopped anger flaring up and gave tempers time to settle.

The Friendly Observer

A lord could pick a person he trusted most, someone fair and honest. He would give them a position in which they constantly observed the lord and when they felt he was on the wrong path they would freely advise him. This was a form of self-check system. However, accounts of samurai remonstrating a lord do say that it should be done in a nice and easy way.

The Changing Samurai Army

The samurai and their value of weapons went through different stages. First, importance was on the bow, then the spear, then the gun and then the sword. But also, the original samurai were more of a mounted archer than a sword fighter, and early samurai forces were used to squash rebellions. These early samurai would charge out in smaller bands and race on horseback across the country, tracking down bandits or rebels (who could be other factions of samurai). They were lightning fast and shot from horseback. Later in the middle ages the armies became massive and more static. They tended to be centralised and on foot, striking at other bases of power. These later armies also had to conscript *ronin* (samurai that didn't belong to a house) and peasants to fill their ranks in times of war.

EARLY SAMURAI   **MIDDLE AGES SAMURAI**

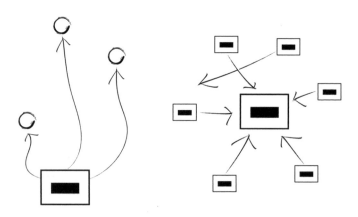

A Return to Virtue

Samurai faced ever-decreasing landholdings as they had to split them between the generations and resorted to selling off sections. This became so bad that a law was passed and land was reverted back to its original owner, with almost no recompense to the 'new' tenant. However, there is more to this than meets the eye when assessing it from the standpoint of Japanese culture.

From a spiritual point of view, the clan who originally owned the land had a connection to it via the dead. Family ancestors who lived and died in that clan residence continued to exist there as ghosts in the eyes of the samurai. The Japanese performed ancestor worship and believed that the dead continued to look over the family, but if the family had sold up and moved on, it caused problems. Therefore, a return to ancestral land was deemed important for the spiritual welfare of Japan, and for families to be severed from their lands was, quite simply, just not proper. This move to bring the original samurai owners back to their ancestral land was called 'a return to virtue'.

The problem that came from this was the fact that the 'new' owners may have been in possession of the land for a long time, maybe 100 years or so, which meant that their ancestors also were born and died in that land.

In addition to this, the question rose of who had rights over that year's crop. Remember, the whole structure was based on crop production, so the value of the crop was massive, as it supported the whole clan, and land did not have value in the way we give it today.

This system, in the end, was considered a failure and was another step towards the fall of the samurai.

Get off My Land!

It is apparent that one problem in the world of the samurai was the stealing of others' land. At some points, samurai families would take or steal land to enlarge their incomes. If you think about it, that is all that samurai war was based on – one clan stealing another clan's land – but when done on a massive scale it was called samurai warfare. On a smaller scale it became a lesser issue, but it is apparent that it was a problem in old Japan. Sometimes, alliances had to be formed to take back the land.

The Snowstorm Raid

The powerful warlord Oda Nobunaga, who also was one of the first to lords reunify Japan, was a 'supporter' of the shogun, meaning that he wanted to use him for his own assent to power. During Nobunaga's rise, there was a time when his puppet-shogun was in danger of being killed and he was surrounded by enemies. It was a three-day ride to the shogun's aid but Nobunaga did it in two. What makes this more impressive is that there was a great snowstorm and some of his men died because of the conditions. Imagine, a company of samurai thundering through a blizzard to bring war to the enemies of the shogun.

Restricted Access

Oda Nobunaga, in his rise to power, prevented some samurai from seeing the shogun in person. By restricting access to the shogun, he stopped any form of loyalty from developing and maintained actual power while the shogun and the emperor were merely figureheads.

The Shogun is Not Always the Shogun

We often hear the word shogun and consider him to be the ruler of Japan, but this may not be so straightforward. Etiquette stated that a shogun was called *kubo* or *kubo-sama* when not at war, and when at war he became the shogun. Also, famous leaders in Japan such as Hideyoshi were not allowed to be called shogun because of their ancestry. Furthermore, early uses of the word shogun simply meant leader of a military force, not leader of the nation, so when thinking of the shogun, do not just think of the single elite ruler at the top, but remember that there were only certain situations where the word shogun was used.

The warrior Aketchi who killed the warlord Nobunaga was known as *mikka-kubo* – the three-day ruler (notice it says *kubo* not shogun).

Samurai and Changing Times

The relationship samurai had with their overlords changed as time progressed. At first, samurai owed their lords a set amount of military service proportional to their situation, meaning that a samurai might have to fight a specific amount of days per year. As time progressed, the samurai held less and less control over their own lands and were forced into castle towns, so instead of an exchange of service they came under the total control of their overlords, and finally under the total control of the shogun of all Japan, changing them from landowning gentry with autonomy to subdued servants under a system of total obedience.

Samurai Carry Three Swords

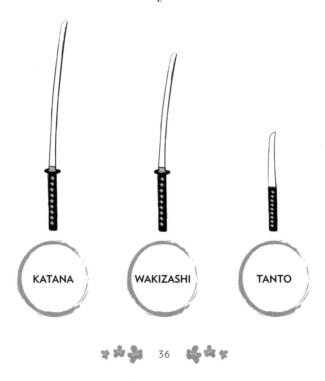

KATANA   WAKIZASHI   TANTO

Often, the samurai were said to carry two swords as a symbol of their status; however, in actuality, they might carry three. Some accounts state that the third blade was a small dagger. This could be either a secret blade hidden on the person or a third, openly worn in armour. It also could be a hidden dagger that was positioned below the tassets of armour when in combat, used for surprise attacks.

A Sword Was Only Drawn for Bloodshed

One common myth about the samurai is that their swords have to taste blood when they had been drawn. This is only a legend, but it does have a very real foundation. Ancient customs say that a samurai's sword, if given new, had to be tested in battle – if there was one to be found – and must be bathed in blood. This does not mean it could not be put back in its sheath if taken out; it means that it had to be tested. Likewise, in normal Japanese society, samurai swords were only drawn if there was a state of combat or if fighting was about to erupt. The samurai warrior named Natori Masazumi tells us that, when a samurai has drawn a sword, it is extremely difficult to settle a situation, so they must think carefully before they draw. He also says that, even if they have drawn their swords, they can replace them before combat starts if an agreement is met. As such, when thinking of samurai, remember that they could take out their blade to clean it, to use it for a test cutting or to show a friend in private, and it could be returned without blood. But for most cases, a sword stayed in its sheath unless a fight was to start and blood was to flow.

The Black Samurai

The now *almost* famous Yasuke was the first black samurai. His story is shrouded in mystery, or at least in a lack of records, but he is considered to have been real and there is little doubt that he existed. It was in the 1580s that a black man came to Japan with the Portuguese. He was shown at court and asked to show his skin and to test if the 'blackness' could be washed off, to check if he was a fake. After it was proven that black skin was a real thing, he was admired and given a position within Nobunaga's army and was considered high ranking. He is thought to have spoken in Japanese and fought in Japanese battles in the warring periods, and was most likely delivered to the Jesuits when the Oda clan fell. Yasuke and other non-Japanese samurai are quickly becoming popular in legend.

The English Samurai

Many people know of William Adams, the first Englishman to get to Japan in 1600. His story is marvellous and he went from being a naval ship's pilot (navigator) to being not only the first English samurai but also a great lord (*hatamoto*) who was given the governance of a place called Hemi. From that time until the decline of the samurai in 1868, Hemi had sent a daily quota of fish to Edo (Tokyo) – a practice that lasted over 250 years.

The Dangerous Boys' Club

Sometimes, samurai were not allowed to form certain private groups and organisations. It was deemed that if too many got together regularly then they might start to form ideas and political aspirations, so groups at some points in history were controlled.

The Way of the Samurai in Peace

After the year 1600, Japan started to become settled and the samurai needed a new way of thinking, so education and refinement became paramount. A samurai of importance called Yamazaki Ansai said the following:

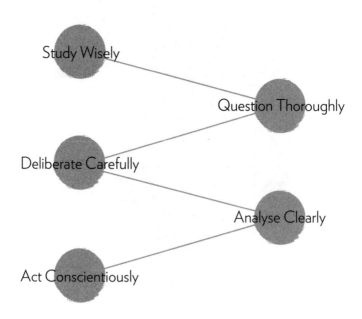

Study Wisely

Question Thoroughly

Deliberate Carefully

Analyse Clearly

Act Conscientiously

The Mongol Invasion

Many people know that the famous kamikaze pilots of the Second World War are named so because the word *kamikaze* means 'divine wind' or 'god-wind' or 'the winds of the gods', but some do not know that the word was used when the Mongols first invaded Japan. In the year 1279, the Mongol fleet came to the shores of Japan and engaged the Japanese samurai in a single day of fighting. The Japanese samurai were actually surprised by the difference in their warfare tactics and the use of gunpowder. However, the Mongol fleet was ravaged by a typhoon and the invasion was stopped. The second invasion came in 1281, when the Mongols took over some islands and enslaved and butchered the people, and from this launch point they engaged in a week-long battle along the Japanese shoreline. This time the samurai were more prepared and there was hellish fighting – 'Mongol versus Samurai' – and with new defences in place the samurai pushed them back to the islands. Again, the *kamikaze* winds came and destroyed the Mongol fleet. It is said that 30,000 Mongol warriors perished at the edge of katana blades with no way of retreat. What is not known is who would have won if it were not for the divine winds that kept out invaders. These natural events helped support the idea that Japan was a place where living gods roamed the Earth in the form of the emperor, and the word *kamikaze* was used to repel foreign invaders in the twentieth century.

Fief Versus Stipend

Most samurai would have a fief and fiefdom, which means that they would own lands, passing them on each generation, and in return they would give military service. Later, this changed to a stipend which is a form of salary based on land production. Samurai were moved to castle towns to live as soldiers rather than as landed gentry, and they were given a salary for their military service, which they passed on to their children. Of course, this diminished in value as more descendants were born, leading to financial problems for the samurai.

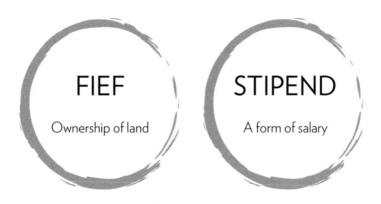

FIEF
Ownership of land

STIPEND
A form of salary

Look, No Hands

Japanese horse reins were actually two pieces of cloth, one attached to each side and held in the right and left hands; in this manner they directed the horse. When going to battle, they tied them together and rode hands-free so that they could use a gun, bow or spear.

Poor Horsemen

One Western account of the samurai and their weapons is given by Bernardino de Avila Giron, who states that Japanese horses are not good enough to do anything but carry firewood and that the samurai are terrible horsemen compared to those in the West. He states that the samurai walk around in a haughty manner but are masters of being humble when they meet other warriors. He goes on to say that they do not shoot so well with bows, and nock the arrows from the opposite side of the bow. He is not at all disrespectful to the courage or fighting skill of the samurai, but he feels their horsemanship leaves something to be desired.

The Atheist Lord

One of the most famous samurai lords of all time is Oda Nobunaga; he stormed through the country in a form comparable to the Blitzkrieg, taking control of Japan. But for a medieval samurai he was very much a pragmatist and, while possibly rude, he was forward-thinking. Travelling with at least 2,000 men when venturing out, he did not believe in the soul or an afterlife or creation by intelligent design. Taking that into consideration, eyewitness accounts tell that Nobunaga tried to create a temple of worship based on himself, making him divine and the centre of all worship for Japan. He was, however, betrayed by one of his generals and forced to commit suicide in a burning temple.

Destruction of the Idols

Oda Nobunaga reformed the way castles were built in Japan. Normally, they had massive earthwork bases and were constructed out of wood. While some stone was used, Nobunaga set out to build a vast complex based on stone foundations. Because this had not been done on such a scale before, there was no infrastructure for it, so he had stone idols and alters destroyed to build his foundations of power, to the horror of the locals who saw their very sacred treasures being smashed up and used.

What It Meant to Be Samurai

The following passage was written in 1159 and outlined just what the samurai did:

> For 7 generations since receiving the name Minamoto, through our skill with the bow and with the transmission of warfare strategy we have until this day put a stop to all rebels and outlaws.

School Yard Cocksurety

It is often a pastime of our society to endow the past samurai with grace, poise, elegance, maturity and wisdom. That is, until they got into a pride match about who should walk down a street first. Around New Year, many of the warlords would visit the shogun. In normal times they would usually have thirty men as a retinue but in this situation they would walk out with 100. The walkways were filled with a mass of people vying to see who had right of way against whom and which lord was most senior. When people of equal rank met, neither would back down, and while it is said the samurai themselves did not join in the jostling, they put their lower servants in front to engage in a pushing match to see which retinue had dominance, until they ended up brawling in defence of their clan and master. The streets of Edo at this time were a mass of cocksure lords, whose servants would fight till they gained the upper hand.

The *Ronin*

Many are familiar with the word *ronin*: a samurai who belongs to no house or has no position. One way of writing *ronin* is 'wave person', meaning 'those who float in the sea of society' and the other is 'person of prison', at which we can guess the meaning. It is said in travellers' accounts that by the end of the period of peace, *ronin*, who still were of high-ranking birth yet had no position and honour, often turned to very dark deeds to secure at least a reputation, and that scars were badges of honour, and a reputation for warrior prowess was held in high regard. For example, one *ronin*, who had committed eighteen murders and had been crucified, had two spears thrust into his side. He then said, in poetic style (literally in a poem), 'the world means nothing to me, do as you wish'. Another *ronin* decided he was going to cut down as many pine trees as possible, to the horror of the Japanese, who love them. In 1861, 600 *ronin* started to threaten foreigners and burn down the port city of Yokohama (which was populated by Westerners at the time). The government had to send troops in and have steamers on standby; the issue was a part of the rising disturbances in Japan as the end of the samurai neared.

First Son for Business, Other Sons for War

When Japanese culture and the problem of the vagabond *ronin* was being explained to the diplomat Henry Heusken in the 1800s, the Japanese explained that the eldest son was brought up to rule over the whole family and that the other sons studied the ways of war. This led to there being many samurai with no official position but who studied war, some of whom became scoundrels who caused crime.

Not All Samurai Are Born Equal

You could be forgiven for thinking all samurai were born equal. In fact, there was a level of pedigree and elitism among the samurai. There were both ancient families and 'new blood'. A samurai could be from an old and noble family, similar to European dynasties, or from lesser houses which served older lines. Moreover, they could be raised from peasant stock to become warriors. At some points in Japanese history, great families were overthrown and the 'new blood' took control. The unifier of Japan, Toyotomi Hideyoshi, is a great example of this. Even he, with his total and absolute authority over Japan, could not be named shogun because his blood was not of ancient stock.

Restricted Power

The history of who and who could not be a samurai, or indeed what actually made someone a samurai, is quite complex. The popular image of the samurai comes from the end of their era, when social movement was very difficult and the idea that you had to be born a samurai comes into play. However, at different periods the barriers between what was samurai and what was not samurai were much looser. As time passed, restrictions were put in place on who could and who could not be samurai and also how far some samurai could rise. There was even a code on which weapons or types of weapons warriors could use, and by the 1600s the peasant class had been stopped from carrying military weapons altogether. (However, they could still carry a short sword.)

Weapons of Power

Even the samurai were restricted in the style of weapons they could carry. There were regulations on the types of handle decoration for spears (silver/white being for a lord) and only the bravest samurai could use a blade with a red-painted groove. Certain banners were regulated and each banner had different meanings, such as the image of a bundle of straw. The straw bundle banner is said to have 100 stalks of straw in it and it represented the 100 great deeds that were to be performed by the warrior. Similarly, the image of a boar meant that the warrior would charge forth. Such banners and weapons had regulations as to who could and could not use them.

Fight to the Death

History tells us that the samurai were not the perfect warriors of virtue, as in fact they were ruthless, deceptive, political, at times traitorous and violent. But old records from those Westerners who met real samurai often say they were indeed fearless, intrepid, loyal and ready to die. While we have to keep one foot in reality, we can still imagine a warrior culture where the men were brought up to fight to the death, to value honour above all things and to lay down their lives for their masters, and while this was not the case for all samurai, many were exemplifiers of the way of the warrior.

The Foot of Doom

To place the foot on another person in Japan is a grave dishonour to give, as is to point with the foot or to kick something. The samurai known as Kamakura Gongoro received an arrow to the face, after which his comrades held him down and tried to withdraw it. However, the arrow was stuck firm, so the warrior withdrawing the arrow had to place his foot on the other's face to pull the arrow out, for which Gongoro became violently angry and swore to take revenge for such an insult. For generations, the episode was told within his clan as a statement of clan honour and bravery.

Plucky Samurai

The Japanese had a very distinct hairstyle called the *chonmage*, and they also wore shaped moustaches and beards; before they started to shave these they would pluck them instead. As most samurai plucked their hair to what we consider to be baldness, it must have been a painful experience. However, towards the end of the 1500s they replaced this custom with shaving.

CHONMAGE

It is thought that the *chonmage* was designed to allow soldiers to pull their hair out of the top of earlier-style helmets so that it did not get too hot, and that after this it became fashion. The name *chonmage* means 'small bun' but the ideograms have changed over time.

A Samurai for the People

There was once a samurai called Masayuki who was so good to his people that he was known as 'an enlightened ruler'. He helped prevent poverty and created a low-interest lending system to allow people to start up their own farms or get through tough times.

The Ambassador of Death

Once the Duke of Satsuma sent an embassy to another lord. The ambassador, being rude in the presence of that lord, was killed by one of his samurai retainers. Instead of killing the whole embassy and simply having done with the matter, the samurai in question later committed suicide on the beach in front of the embassy party. This was done so that the incident did not become political and troublesome. Both sides accepted this and life continued as normal.

The Spear of Office

The diplomat Henry Heusken said that high-level officials (*bugyo*) would walk with a spear bearer before them, showing the public that they were officers of the shogun. He also said that the ultimate goal of an officer was to be allowed to wear the crest of the Tokugawa family and that in Japan it was an honour for anyone of an inferior position to be allowed to wear the crest of a senior clan.

The Royal 'We'

According to Henry Heusken, at his meeting with the shogun of Japan, the shogun did not use personal pronouns such as 'I', as he was too grand to use such words that made him a person.

BALD EAGLE

Eagles were kept in small wooden houses inside rich palaces. These tame birds had their feathers plucked out so they could be used as arrow flights for wealthy samurai.

The Not-So-Brave Samurai

Mitford records that at the end of the time of the samurai he was not convinced about their valour or bravery, saying that all attacks on people or forces from the West at that point had been sneaking ambushes and not outright confrontation.

The English Guard in Japan

In Yokohama in the 1800s, the British Army stood 'side by side' with samurai. These English soldiers were from the 9th Regiment, also known as the Norfolks, and they protected Mitford, but alongside these guards were also samurai. However, some of these samurai, while acting as guards, were also spies for the government.

The Bugle in Japan

In the town of Yokohama, in the later period of the samurai, you would hear the wake-up call, or reveille (spelt as 'rewelly' in the original document), of the English soldiers stationed there. Each morning the English bugles would sound out around the town.

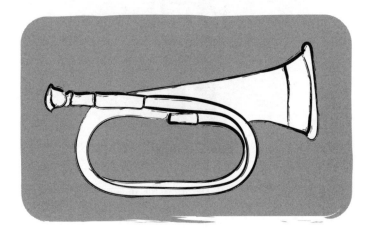

The English-style Guards of Japan

Everyone in the world knows of the Queen's Guards in London, with red coat and black hat, who stand motionless and erect, not allowed to say a word unless threatened or challenged. Well, the same holds for the samurai guards in old Japan. A guard on duty (according to American diplomats in the 1800s) would stand 'erect and motionless' and bow to no one who passed save for the *ometsuke* – the overseer.

Furthermore, Natori Masazumi, in his ancient scrolls, says that a castle guard should use six weapons.

番所六具之事
Bansho Rokugu no Koto
The six tools for guard duty:

Hayanawa 早縄 – quick-rope for binding
Kumade 熊手 – the bear-claw staff
Tsukubo 突棒 – spiked T-bar staff
Hyoshigi 拍子木 – wooden warning clappers
Bo 棒 – quarterstaff
Sasumata 指胯 – U-shaped pronged staff

More information like the above can be found in the *Book of Samurai* series.

 54

There is Noble and There is Noble

We often think of the samurai as warriors of the nobility, but this is not the case. Some samurai were noble and some were not. To be of the nobility you had to descend from a royal line, but to be a samurai you did not have to be royalty. This means that there was a basic split among samurai: those of royal blood and those not. Some samurai were close relatives of the emperor and some samurai were just excellent warriors who had had a battlefield promotion. When talking about the samurai, do not mix them up with court nobles and the imperial line; the samurai served the nobility, but as time progressed the two became mixed.

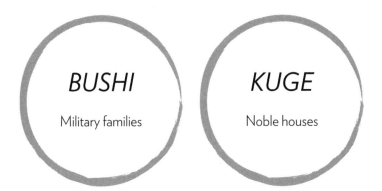

BUSHI

Military families

KUGE

Noble houses

The Last and Lonely Shogun

The title Shogun of Japan came to refer to overall military ruler of the country and there was no one higher than him in the land save the emperor; even then the actual power was with the samurai. Even the last shogun before his fall had hundreds of spearmen follow him everywhere – great warlords held their faces to the floor, hands on knees, and no one had as many people bow and scrape before them. However, at a banquet dinner in 1906, Mitford spoke to the then ex-shogun about their old times together, in the dangerous days of civil war, but Mitford lamented when, at the end of the evening, the ex-shogun was driven away without a single groom or man in attendance. He simply went back to his home without any pomp and ceremony – something that years ago would have been a full parade but was now just one lonely man and the last of a forgotten age.

The Great Lords

Many samurai enthusiasts know the word *daimyo*, which was a position in Japan that equates to baron or regional warlord. However, early in samurai history, this was most likely pronounced as *taimai*.

The Types of Japanese Disembowelment

The three types of *seppuku* recorded by Mitford in the 1800s were:

1. The suicide of a high-ranking warrior in prison. He was surrounded by four guards and two execution officers and was only allowed a wooden dagger. As he reached for it, his head was taken by one officer and presented by the other.

2. The suicide of a warlord's retainer. As above, he was surrounded by four guards and two execution officers. In this instance, he was allowed a real dagger and stabbed himself, and the officer on his left cut off his head while the one on the right presented the head.

3. The suicide of a warlord. This was said to be done in his own grounds and was reported to the shogun afterwards. If the offence was great, half of his property was taken; if minor then the property was inherited intact. Interestingly, Mitford stated that in this form of execution, the condemned cut his throat, not the belly.

Most of my previously published research on *seppuku* has been translated from Japanese manuals. However, this account was compiled by Mitford on hearing about it during his time among the samurai, and we know for a fact that he did see *seppuku* first-hand.

Hardcore Suicide

One story of ferocious suicide tells of a young man who cut open his belly three times horizontally, then twice vertically and then, taking his dagger out, thrust it sideways through his neck – blade edge to the front – then, with both hands on the blade and a gritting of teeth, cut out his own throat and died.

The Story of Yui Shosetsu

One of my favourite warriors in Japanese history is Yui Shosetsu, admittedly because he is connected to Natori-Ryu, which is the school of samurai warfare I study, but also because he seems to have been a natural talent. He is considered as one of the Three Great *Ronin* and was an expert martial artist and a high-level strategist. Much of his life is speculation, and so I knowingly use the words 'it is said'. Thus, it is said that he was a student of the great war master Kusunoki Fuden, and that he married his daughter, but although Kusunoki was his master and father-in-law, he poisoned him and stole his secret scrolls, taking over his students. It is not known if this is true, but what is known is that he set up a martial academy in Tokyo and taught martial arts and military strategy from there and had a very successful school and myriad students. The surprising thing is that he is said to have not been born a samurai, as he was a common man in a time of strict social control, but was so good that he became a *ronin* and in the end had samurai followers. He is also said to have been invited to be a guest and friend of the warlord of Kishu domain, Tokugawa Yorinobu (the son of Tokugawa Leyasu) and that together they formed a plot to overthrow the shogun. This was called the Keian Uprising. The plot was discovered and Yui

Shosetsu committed suicide, and the lord of Kishu was put under house arrest. However, as stated, often fact and fiction are mixed together and there is still plenty of research to be done on this interesting man. But what is almost certain is his connection to Natori-Ryu, the samurai school of war – a samurai school that created one of the most famous ninja scrolls of all time which has been translated and published in English as *True Path of the Ninja*, and it is possible that much of this ninja information comes from Yui Shosetsu and his amazing rise to fame.

The Reality of War

We are all familiar with post-traumatic stress, with the reality of death and of military conflict, and the effects it has on people. Some soldiers find it hard to readjust, some become hardened to violence and their minds move outside of social norms, even if they remain functional and controlled in society, while others move into the private sector and have a love for war and combat. It is with this reality that we must see the samurai warrior, not through the lens of historical fantasy but through the reality that life at war brings. But only a certain percentage of the samurai actually went to battle or actually killed other men in combat. There were great times of peace and great times of war. Some samurai were simply hardened by combat and killing, bringing them as humans to investigate moral codes or to value life; others who did not have that experience of war concentrated on *bushido*, the military codes of the samurai. They developed ways of doing things, strong ritual and brotherly bonds. Eventually the idea of following a philosophical way was built upon in twentieth-century martial arts, such as aiki-do, ju-do, karate-do, kyu-do, etc. This idea of a 'way' found in the later samurai times found its way to modern Japanese arts. Often, these arts do not truly represent ways of war, but their foundation was set a long time ago when the samurai were at battle, and as years of peace followed, they found their way into the modern Japanese ethical system, making the 'soul of the samurai' present to this day.

The Shadow Servant

When Japan was taken over by the Tokugawa family, each lord had to spend 50 per cent of his time in the capital. The diary of Richard Cocks, who was in Japan in the early 1600s, tells us that when these lords were 'in town' they would be accompanied by one of the shogun's men who would be in the position of a servant to them. These men then reported everything back to the government and acted as an informant.

The One-Use Cup

If a lord was travelling and stayed at the castle of another samurai or at another family's manor house, sometimes cups were specially commissioned just for that stay. These cups had clan crests on them or other such symbols. After the cup was used by the visiting lord, it would never be used again; instead it was kept as an heirloom to be passed on for generations.

The Decline of the Samurai

It is often remarked that from the year 1600 the samurai fell into decline. Without war to temper them in combat they became bureaucrats and accountants; they became soft and weak. This is often supported by the need for people of lesser ranks to be recruited as fighters in the 1868 restoration of the emperor and the fall of the samurai class. I would not disagree with this statement, and I too feel that the warlike perfection of the earlier samurai had indeed faded through the Edo period and that a samurai from the period of wars may have been somewhat surprised at the calibre of the samurai of later days. However, it does not mean that society at the end of samurai times only consisted of weak and useless warriors. In fact, there were some samurai who were dedicated to war and there were plenty of ruffians and *ronin* who would be ready to jump to violence. In fact, the idea of the samurai laying down his life for honour may have been more present at the end of samurai times than the start. There were always samurai who would fight to the death, from AD 800 to the 1800s, no matter how poor they had become in their duties as war masters.

One recurring feature of Victorian accounts of Tokyo is that it could be a dangerous place. While it was very well regulated and probably a safe place to spend your days, certain areas and night-time quarters attracted hot-blooded young men, drunk on both wine and tales of old, who would fight it out, and the dawn would bring news of another death. The accounts also record that when a person was ready to take action, they would kill anyone of any rank and then kill themselves.

Therefore, while it is agreed that the overall level of the collective samurai did decline in later times, there were enough individuals to make cities in Japan dangerous places, and a society that raised its men – no matter what level of combat skill they had – on tales of old and of heroic death, produced men ready to die for honour. These individuals were numerous enough to show the Western visitor that you never messed with a samurai or his honour.

The Last Samurai

If you ask most people who have an interest in samurai history 'when did the period of the samurai end?', they will often answer 1868 and they would not wholly be incorrect. However, it might be better to ask when did the samurai class *start* to come to an end? Then the answer truly would be 1868. If you could travel to 1869 you would still see samurai here and there, still as samurai and still enjoying samurai culture in many ways. On 25 July 1869, the Japanese government officially changed the samurai into two classes, the *shozoku* which meant 'warrior families' and the *kazoku* which became 'noble families', the latter being of higher level. The samurai rule was an outdated system that was highlighted by Western trade requests. This led to a war in which the shogun's rule was overthrown, after which the emperor became the true head of state again (with little power) and the samurai lost control of their lands and their structure for payment. After this, they were given the status of *shozoku* and *kazoku* to separate them from common folk, but after the Second World War the government revised this and in 1946 and 1947 the titles were dropped and Japanese people became universally equal.

Therefore, if asked 'when did the samurai end?', you can say their end started in 1868 but they truly ended and were phased out by 1947.

The Last True Samurai

As samurai ways came to an end in the second half of the 1800s and eventually faded out after almost 1,000 years of service, it is moving to read an eyewitness description in English by people who were actually there at the end-times with the last of the samurai before they became *shizoku* (warrior familes):

> Their war jackets were not unlike those of our herald's tabards, were as many in colour as Joseph's coat. Hideous masks of lacquer and iron, fringed with portentous whiskers and moustaschious, crested helmets with wigs from which long streamers of horse-hair floated to their waists, might strike terror into an enemy. They looked like hobgoblins of a nightmare.

Mitford, 1868

Japanese Society

The Battle for the Soul of the East

As the samurai era moved through its final quarter, new Western ideas and a more modern approach was starting to infiltrate the land. In the 1500s, guns and Western armour had come to Japan, changing warfare considerably, and later Dutch science started to seep in through the limited trade that was still allowed. Medical and scientific thinking started to change, and the country began to divide into those who believed in the old Japanese ways and those who saw the accuracy of modern Western thinking. This movement truly started to shape modern Japan and is one reason why, when the Americans arrived in the 1800s, Japan was ready to divide between keeping the old ways and opening up to the world.

Sir Isaac Newton

The first time Sir Isaac Newton's work was translated into Japanese was 1777.

The Calendar

The Japanese calendar is the same as the Chinese calendar, and both are different from the Western calendar. As you will have noticed, the Western New Year starts on 1 January but each year Chinese New Year changes its start date. This is because they have to calculate the correct day based on the movement of both the moon and the sun. Sometimes they have to add days to the year or even an extra month, just to make sure it aligns. This means that each year the start date has to be calculated and then told to the people.

Samurai in Charge of the National Calendar

Samurai not only took charge of the security of the country, but many families had professions that they carried on for generations. The Chinese calendar used in Japan needed to be calculated each year and it was the job of two samurai families to make sure the nation had the correct astronomical calculations. This meant that the two major warrior households not only studied warfare and interacted with samurai politics, but most of their time was spent on the study and recording of the stars and the movement of the heavens, almost like astronomer-warriors. However, a low-ranking person from out of nowhere reformed the way the Japanese looked at the heavens, with a more modern approach that took away much of their power with this new way of thinking; he was made a samurai for his efforts.

Peasant Uprisings

Most village documents have been destroyed and many records were lost. However, statistics show that between 1600 and 1868 there were approximately 3,000–5,000 peasant uprisings, making it around twenty per year across all of Japan. Some of them were violent, some very organised. This is why I often have an issue with the Tokugawa Period (1600–1868) being known as the period of peace, because in this time there were the siege of Osaka Castle, the Shimabara Rebellion, the Keian Uprising, the Boshin War and, of course, up to 5,000 peasant revolts. However, the land was actually at peace in comparison to the period of wars.

The Rule of Men

Men in old Japan were often legally free to have sex with prostitutes or lower-class women, but wives were not allowed to sleep with other men. Some classes of women could be killed for simply talking to another man (but remember we are talking about a 1,000-year period so things changed from time to time).

Muddy Waters

There is a form of short analogy in Japan that is based on the idea of muddy water. It is said that if the water flow at the surface level is cloudy, dirty and unclear, it means the water above the riverbed is also stained. This means that if the ruler is not pure, the people will also be corrupt, but if the ruler is pure then the people will follow suit, and therefore society should not be like muddy water.

Stubbornness Versus Steadfastness

One chronicler witnessed some Christians being martyred by being held over a waterfall that fell into hot sulphur water from a natural spring. The place was nicknamed 'hell'. He said that even when they were held over the edge they did not recant their faith and so were pushed to their death in the boiling water below. He made the observation that perhaps Japanese society promoted stubbornness instead of steadfastness. He came to this conclusion because the people who were being tortured did not actually know much about Christianity itself; they were actually being stubborn about their right to those beliefs and not the beliefs themselves. This is a complex social question but it is worth thinking about.

The First Dissection of a Human Body

While the Japanese used to cut up bodies for fun to test *katana*, they did not start medically dissecting bodies until 1771. They did this to test the validity of Dutch anatomy charts, and the first proper dissection was performed on an old lady who sold tea in Kyoto. The Japanese were astonished at how accurate these medical charts were, and Western medicine gained more of a foothold.

Price-Rigging

In the period of peace towards the end of samurai times, the merchants really came into power and it is said they communicated with each other and rigged prices up and down the country, maintaining good profits for all. Their power was becoming so great that real strife had become evident between the warriors and the merchants.

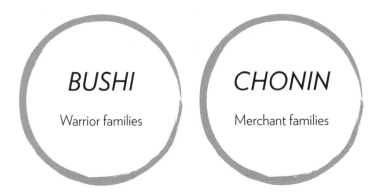

BUSHI

Warrior families

CHONIN

Merchant families

Universal Texts

In the early, more unified times, Japanese society concentrated on a pursuit of Buddhist literature and teachings, with a focus around the court in Kyoto. During the turbulent times in the 1400s and 1500s things began to change, and in the new, unified Japan of the post 1600s they focused on neo-Confucianism. Both times of unity focused on a set of ideals; one swayed more towards Buddhist teachings, the other to the words of Confucius. Japan has always been a mix of religions.

Skin Disease

One common factor that continually repeats itself in foreign accounts of the Japanese is poor skin or skin disease. Today it is reversed; I would say the Japanese have great skin in the modern world and gauging the age of a Japanese person can be difficult. Medieval accounts say that there were sores and scabs and skin problems seen on many of the people. Other accounts state that leprosy was quite common in Japan.

Travel advice said that you should bathe in an inn during the day, because the Japanese bathe after they have worked. This way the traveller would have got clean, 'virgin' water to bathe in before the guests and locals made it filthy.

Stifle That Racket

Western chroniclers state that the music of the Japanese is discordant and screechingly bad to listen to. They claim it is not as harmonious as Western music, but that it is a discordant wail and all Japanese sing together in a painful cacophony.

Japanese music can be an acquired taste, but once acquired the discordant sound is sweet, and a trip to a Japanese event accompanied by music can bring a smile to one's face.

Squeeze One Out

Japanese women about to give birth, and who were used to wearing their wide sashes quite loose, were bound up extremely tightly, so much so that it almost flattened their belly. They did this because they said that it helped avoid birthing complications.

Japanese Prisons

One Westerner who found himself in a Japanese prison said it was a wooden room that was boarded up tight so that very little light entered and the prisoners lived in a constant dimness. It was 33 feet long, 12 feet wide and quite low. Everyone was stripped to a loin cloth and positioned in rows. The heat was unbearable in summer and it was rat-filled in winter (but apparently still warm in winter because there were so many people).

Eradicating History

When Christianity was banned in Japan, the churches, burial grounds and living quarters of all the Christians were taken down, removed, or lived in by native priests, the idea being to eradicate all trace of the then banned religion.

Carry Me Across the River

In Japan, there was a tradition of people who carried others across the river, acting as a form of water taxi by giving piggybacks over narrow places. However, if there had been too much rainfall a person could be stuck at these crossing points for days, waiting for the water level to fall enough to be carried across.

Japanese Rice

Some forms of Japanese rice were actually imported from South East Asia and were only then produced on a large scale in Japan, thus becoming Japanese rice.

PICK A WINNER

Western people pick their nose with their index finger or thumb but Japanese people pick it with their little finger because they tend to have tiny nostrils.

The Silence of the Masses

One of the great wonders of Japan, even to this day, is the silence that is maintained by mass populations of people. Standing on a train in central Tokyo, surrounded by hundreds of people, you can travel in pure silence for all of your journey, until the doors open to the noise of the crowded station (which is often the sound of the singing tannoy system and the artificial chirping birds). Likewise, in the 1800s when diplomat Henry Heusken's procession moved through the streets of Edo, he claimed that, in truth, there must have been 1 million people lining the streets to see the American ambassadors pass through, and they did so in pure silence with looks of interest on their faces. Edo was one of the first cities to reach 1 million people, and while the 1 million may not have been there, an immense congregation must have been, and with typical Japanese obedience, there was silence.

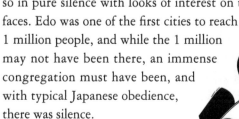

The Japanese Domesday Book

In 1590, Toyotomi Hideyoshi carried out a massive survey of his lands, asking the man doing the survey to leave no field unchecked, lest he have to do the job himself. So thorough was his job – and the consequent surveys that followed over the next seventy-five years – it raised the production of that land by 80 per cent. It is unknown if this was just a case of tax being increased or the survey had highlighted lands and villages that had become defunct and were thus populated again and the fields worked to bring in crops; it was most likely a mixture of the two. The land surveys started in the dark days of the warring periods, when deserted villages, overgrown meadows and unused land was abundant, and it transformed the area into a mapped out, heavily taxed, structured population who used the land better and to a higher output. This allows us to see how the period of peace after 1600 started to make a new Japan and the old ways of the age of wars came to an end.

The More the Merrier

One move made in the mid 1600s was to have more independent farmsteads that were smaller in size instead of fewer that were larger in size. The reason for this is that independent farm holders had the right to control their own land, marry whom they liked, and other such benefits. It was deemed – and correctly so – that people in charge of and responsible for their own land would work harder and be more productive than people working for someone else. This created much happier, smaller and more productive units. However, the system did not fit into how the land tax was calculated, and if the calculations on production were too high, or if there was a famine, then these farmsteads could not produce enough money. The result of this was the collapse of these independent holdings, and their owners came to be known as 'broken farmers'.

Broken Farmers

After surveys were taken of the land, starting in the late 1500s and going into the 1600s, tax was often calculated on what the land *should* produce and not what it *did* produce, meaning that tax was calculated on a 100 per cent production rate, and of course no business or land works at 100 per cent efficiency. This meant that some of the smaller farmers could not keep up with the payments and lost their land, while richer farmers became poorer. (Remember, this is the time of the rise of the merchants.) Those farmers who lost their land were known as 'broken farmers' and had to become indentured servants. An indentured servant is a free person who

goes into a contract with another and becomes, in effect, a slave for a specific period of time. This means that the 'broken farmers' would sell themselves to other local farms and their land would lie unused. This, of course, was a compounding problem, because the land was still on the registry as 100 per cent efficient, and the next year taxes would still be demanded, but the actual produce would be lower. This was a spiral of destruction. Therefore, while there was enough land and while there were people willing to farm it, the tax set-up was so one sided that the rules in place stopped them from being able to actually work the land, which in turn created more poor people and less freedom.

Torches and Pitchforks

In the early to mid 1600s, a collection of peasants stormed their lord's castle and killed an official who had been sent there to quell the social unrest due to heavy taxation. One can imagine the burning torches and cries against the tyrant lord. In response, the government became involved and executed 130 peasants and took control of the land due to bad management.

Burn Them Down!

In some cases when the farmers rose up, they went from village to village, collecting people for the revolt. Often, the headman of the village would make the decision to join or not, depending on their own situation. If they said no, the protesters asking for their help often threatened to burn the farms down and kill everyone, which caused a further dimension to the trouble between the various groups.

Off With Their Heads!

There was once a small domain that had stringent taxes. Two prominent farmers distributed leaflets to the area, gathered a large crowd and marched on to the public offices to demand justice. The public officers heard their disputes, looked at the financial situation and agreed that there was indeed reason for leniency and help, and they gave the demanded aid and settled the matter. However, the two who started the uprising were shackled and paraded from village to village and, just where the crowd had gathered, they were executed, even though their appeal was fair and agreed upon. The farmers were in the right, their case peaceful and their protest morally correct, but you simply did not protest against the samurai.

And Don't Do it Again!

In the 1600s, Japan closed its gates to the world and said that any ship coming in would be burnt and its crew killed. In 1640, a trade delegation from Macao was sent to Japan: the ship was burnt and out of the sixty-one crew all were beheaded, apart from thirteen individuals who were ferried back to mainland China, with the warning not to send anyone else.

Angry and Hungry

It is considered impolite to show anger and hunger in Japan. The Japanese value controlled emotion and it is rude to appear hungry. A modern trope of this is found in Japanese films where the lone *ronin* warrior is leaning against a wall, casually looking about – Clint Eastwood style – the warrior has in his mouth a toothpick and he seems calm. The idea of using a toothpick is to display to people you have eaten and that you are not hungry. However, most of the time in such films, the warrior is poor and has no food, but as a warrior he cannot appear to be hungry, so he uses a toothpick. Also, the very fact that you likely understood what I meant by 'Clint Eastwood style' is of interest. You imagine the lone gunman looking dangerous, leaning against a wall, but in truth, Western films got their inspiration from earlier Japanese films on warriors. So next time you see Clint Eastwood or the like standing in the shade, picking at their teeth, know that they are replicating Japanese social politeness.

The Tent Government

At the beginning of the samurai period, Japan was run by the noble class and the samurai served them as military men and in other offices but when the samurai took power they created a military government, called *bakufu*, which is often translated as 'tent government'. The name comes from the curtains that were used in a samurai camp and should be understood as 'battlefield government', meaning 'military rulership'. You will often see these war curtains in samurai movies.

BAKUFU
Tent government

Girls Who Wanted to Be Prostitutes

When the Dutch were locked inside their trading station and not allowed to wander freely, there were a number of locals who wanted to be prostitutes for them. Some girls of 14 or 15 years old would be prostituted, but often the Dutch simply paid them a weekly or monthly salary and had them maintain the house and sleep with them at night. This allowed the girls to save up enough money to be married or to allow them a better start in life, so when their Dutch 'sugar daddy' left Japan, or when they had saved enough, they moved on and started a better life than than they might have originally hoped for. In some cases it was a mutually beneficial situation. We have to be careful here, because the same thing continues to happen in Japan today in a slightly different form. Some schoolgirls in Japan will prostitute themselves out for the ever-growing 'need' for luxury items and they do so voluntarily, so be aware that prostitution in Japan has multiple levels and angles.

The Not-so-lucky Prostitutes

While some women welcomed sexual relationships for money to advance themselves, some were forced into it. Actresses who were on the move from town to town would sometimes be 'pimped' out to people who had seen them in their show. Sadly, when they died, they were wrapped in straw and just tossed into a field, used and unwanted.

Kyoto or Not?

Most people are aware of the city of Kyoto, Japan's city of culture. Some people know that it was once Japan's capital and was the official capital city for 1,000 years but that power was not always centralised there. However, fewer people know that it has had more than one name, one of which is Heian, a term which gives its name to the Heian Period (the late 700s to the late 1100s).

HEIAN IS THE
OLD NAME
FOR KYOTO

Coming of Age

When samurai boys came of age in Japan – about 15 years old – they would be given a set of real swords to distinguish them as men.

Are You Married?

It was easy to tell if a lady was married in old Japan; she would have her teeth stained black with a form of iron ink. They were not rotten teeth; in fact, the dye is said to give some protection against tooth decay. When these blackened teeth are seen against a powdered white face, it can be quite beautiful and was seen by the Japanese as attractive.

I Brought You into this World and I Will Take You Out of It

English parents sometimes say this to their children, but in old Japan this was a reality. Families or clan masters had the right of death over lower family members at certain points in Japanese history. If the head of the family wanted you dead it was not impossible to do. Remember, some parents who were poor used to sell their children into slavery and prostitution. This was not even one of those unused powers. Richard Cocks was in Japan around the year 1600 and his diary claims that he saw such killings.

The Wandering Spellcaster

One broad distinction that can be made is that the wealthy in Japan used highly educated monks who had a base of operation and were well versed in esoteric ways to administer to their spiritual and supernatural needs, while the poor used less-educated wandering spellcasters and shamans to perform the esoteric services needed. This is one reason why there are so many different types of spells and magic used in Japan and esoteric Japanese practices are extremely varied and mixed.

The Two Types of Four Classes

Most people know that there are four classes of people in Japan:

However, one European traveller in Japan in the 1500s (before Japan made social mobility difficult) said that there was an alternative four classes of people:

Most likely this means: noble birth; people who have a profession, such as farmers, merchants, etc.; military men; and then others such as vagabonds, travellers and the mobile.

The Business of Being a Monk

Being a monk is Japan is actually like running a business. Monks are allowed to marry and many of them can eat meat. If they have children, they pass on the task of being a monk to their offspring. Many temples have had the same family running them for hundreds of years. In its own way, it is a family-run business.

The Nobleman's Rise and Shine

An account from AD 960 gives the following ritual for a nobleman about to start his day:

Rise
Chant the name of the star associated with that year
Check yourself in the mirror
Check the date and discover if there are any omens of luck or ill luck
Clean your teeth
Face west; wash your hands and face
Chant the name of the Buddha
Chant the name of the Shinto shrine you are connected to

The Search for the Next Life

It is said that the old people of Japan had no qualms with death and that many actively sought the next life. We see this in suicide in its many forms, but João Rodrigues tells us that some of the Japanese of medieval Japan, on hearing of the beauty and grand splendour of the afterlife, would kill themselves in order to reach this spiritual happiness before their allotted time and to exit the doldrums of this life.

The Japanese are Best – So Say the Japanese

Those people who have spent extended time in modern Japan are left with a very polite but distinct understanding that, if it is Japanese, the Japanese consider it to be correct and, of course, the best. You may be met with a look of distaste if your electronic device is Chinese or Korean, because such lowly and accursed objects cannot in any way compare to the superior Japanese versions. Equally, Japanese rice, oranges, motor cars, robots and all other things are, of course, the best in the world. It is not that others are unservicable; it is just that they are not Japanese. What is interesting is that, in his account from the 1500s, the traveller João Rodrigues states:

> They accordingly have a haughty and proud sprit, and however much they see or hear of other nations, they always think that their country is the best, especially as regards to their weapons and their use of war. They have an intrepid and bold spirit, and they believe that nobody in the whole world equals them in this respect and that all are far inferior to them.

As someone who has lived in Japan for an extended period, I don't think much has changed.

The Merry and the Melancholy

Rodrigues' medieval account tells us that the Japanese disliked trade and perturbing matters. They preferred to enjoy life, to fill their time with merriment and entertainment – being as happy as hobbits – but he also said that they would fall into deep bouts of melancholy and die from an empty and dark heart.

Three Hearts in One

It is said that the Japanese have three hearts:

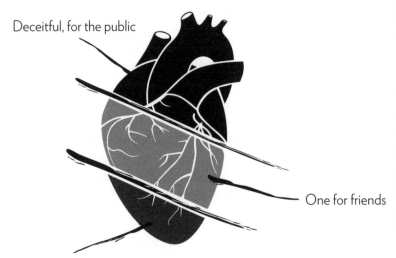

Deceitful, for the public

One for friends

One they never show to anyone

The Japanese are still very much like this: the Japanese have a public face, a semi-private face and one they hide deep down, which only rises in anger or drunkenness.

The Walk of Shame

In the 1870s, there was a woman who was on her way to bathe. She walked across the street to the bath stark naked, as she expected all the men to be away from their small village working. She looked up and saw a Western gentleman, and as their gazes met she stumbled and tried to cover herself and was extremely embarrassed by the situation. There was a strange mix in old Japan of open nakedness – on public paths and in hot springs, for example – but there is also the opposite end of the scale where some women were not even allowed to be seen or talked to. The delicate barriers of society were many and it needs an experienced hand to understand them.

Solid as Gold

The Japanese are fastidious in their honesty over money. Old-time travellers declared that the Japanese were exact in all measurements, weights and exchanges, unlike the thieving medieval Chinese and Koreans. To this day, a Japanese shopkeeper will chase you down the street to return a few pennies of change. Tipping is extremely rare in Japan.

Beards

We often consider the Japanese to be without beards, but this fashion has changed over time. There are many examples in art and accounts which tell us that the Japanese enjoyed various and beautiful styles of facial hair, from beards to moustaches. Different accounts even state that the people of the orient actually influenced Western beard shapes. However, it is said the men of the East very rarely had great big bushy beards.

The Upside-Down Times

In the 1500s, Japan entered the 'upside-down' times, when the samurai of lesser birth and of lower social standing took control of the whole country and created a period of warfare that lasted over 100 years. It is commonly known as the Warring States Period. The upper-class samurai tried to emulate the delicate royalty and left the harder tasks and communication with the people to the lesser samurai, who grew stronger and more powerful, creating an upside-down Japan.

Contemplation and Nostalgia

The Japanese did not dwell on ideas of happiness, but felt that time for thought should be focused on contemplation of life and ideas of nostalgia. For the Japanese, it was best to sit within their rooms, looking at a painting of a seasonal scene, remembering times gone by and considering the meaning of life.

The Drinking Monk

When Christians first started to come to Japan, the Catholics tried to persuade the Buddhist monks about their faith, but one canny monk knew how to beat them. The Catholics continued to invite him to their house and drink alcohol, which he accepted gratefully (many times), and when they told him about the virtue of Christian beliefs he said that his sect also had the very same teachings. Each time they told him a new part of their faith, he replied exactly the same – 'Oh, we have that one too' – and then he would drink more. When they really pressed him on the matter, he said he had a matter to attend to and had to leave. In this manner he continued to get drunk at the expense of the foreigners.

It Is Only a Typhoon

Henry Heusken, in his journal, states that after great storms, with towns laid to waste, ships destroyed and the area ruined, the people of Japan simply started about their repairs, so used to the destruction that they did not even mourn or cry in horror. It was simply the way of Japan.

Women Are Better Shopkeepers

João Rodrigues, in his 1604 account, tells us that the menfolk of Kyoto who ran the businesses actually did not stay in their businesses during the day. Instead, they met with other men to 'do business' of some form and to find pleasures in the city. It was the women who were left with the running of the shops in the day, because men had short and hot tempers and things could get nasty when issues came up for debate. Therefore, he tells us, the more rational women, who could deal with such things, would actually look after the shops.

How Buddhism Entered Japan

We all imagine a Chinese monk walking up the shore of Japan, ready to spread the word of Buddhism, peace and the way to avoid the dangers of the social world. Well, this is actually not very accurate. Buddhism went to Japan in stages and was divided into different sects, many of which hated the others and vied for political power. Later on, after Buddhism was established, different historical figures went to Japan to bring in new waves of Buddhism and establish new political powers. The key was to get the rulers of the nation to subscribe to a specific form of Buddhism, which would bring the power of the support of their followers. In short, Buddhism was actually a political game in a search for power, and some monasteries were extremely powerful, both politically and militaristically. The poor monk wandering Japan spreading the word of a pure life and changing the hearts of a nation is more fantasy than reality.

The Japanese Natives

Known to some, but unfamiliar to others, the Ainu people were the original inhabitants of Japan, before the Japanese themselves. Eyewitness accounts say that they were well built but small, handsome yet strange in appearance. They wore long beards and different clothes to the Japanese. The women coloured their lips blue and had blue rings on the skin of their wrists and wore coloured beads on their neck. Both men and women had broad silver earrings or silks hanging from their ears. The men used the bow, spear and dagger as weapons and sometimes, but not always,

shaped their hair in the same style as the Japanese. However, they did have great long beards which they had to hold up with small fork-like implements as they ate. They had bamboo armour and used arrows tipped with lethal poison. They were prone to drink a lot but not get too drunk, and are said to have loved a good scrap but their fights did not end in death. Their punishment system was less strict than the Japanese in that adultery was punished by removing hair and by other forms of embarrassment, as opposed to the Japanese death sentence for almost anything. It is said they worshipped the gods of the sun, mountains and rivers for protection, and can be considered the last native people of Japan.

The Hard-Working Japanese

The work ethic of the Japanese is famous throughout the world, but it was not always so. In the 1800s the diplomat Heusken fired his groom for 'doing as he pleased' and not performing his job. Japanese documents also warn of hiring attendants in Edo to carry swords, as such attendants would run off with the swords and sell them on the market.

The Blue Headband

There was one band of seafaring people who were bronze in skin colour, wore only a loincloth, and wore a blue headband over their noses as they stood on the prows of their craft in the crystal blue waters.

The Birth of Japanese Style

As the influence of China and the craze for all things Chinese raged across Japan, trade could not fulfil the needs of everyone and there were just not enough Chinese goods. As a result of this, the Japanese pushed their efforts into creating the missing parts of their material culture, and from this lack of goods (among other things) came a rise in 'Japanese style'.

The Last Remnants of Western Style

When Western style made its way to Japan, it took over by storm, in both high and low classes, and even at state dinners the music and entertainment was now Western, including music by composers such as Wagner, Beethoven, Mozart and Rossini. This meant that the lower classes followed suit and young ladies began to learn the piano and the violin, something that was quite normal in Western society in the 1800s. Now, in our modern times, the use of instruments and the learning of music at home is quite rare, but once upon a time, most houses had a piano and some instruments. My stay in Japan in the early 2000s saw the dying echo of this in Japan. I remember sitting in a Kyoto guest house, being entertained by the daughter of the household playing very elegant piano for us. Many times I have visited houses where the daughters in Japan are taught music and recital as a standard. I fear that is now dying away, as it has done in the West, and that experiences like this are an echo of the great trend of adopting Western style and is a direct descendant of those first great balls held by the Emperor of Japan when he entertained Western nobility and royal blood. Soon, even that echo will come to an end, but I hope it will leave a resonance in world history and that people will know that such royal visits caused a gentle wave in society that lasted 100 years or more.

The Shelves of Privilege

Mitford states a curious thing; he says that one form of shelf in a Japanese house was used to reflect the position of the samurai in the household, as hierarchy was very important. He says that the highest ranking would put his things on this high shelf. Thus the highest shelf was reserved for the trappings of the high born.

Prayer for the Dying

In 1107, the emperor was dying at the age of about 29. All types of priests and monks, witch doctors, shamans and spellcasters were called. Each tried to cure the emperor, which would have given them fame and success. They all failed; he died. The end.

The Police Salute

When Townsend Harris and Henry Heusken passed at night under torchlight through the city of Odawara, the police, bearing lanterns on staffs, lined the road and beat those staffs on the ground in salute of the great ambassadors of America. It was a beautiful scene under the clear sky with a gorgeous city sparkling with lights.

Horse and Pony

People often imagine the samurai on massive warhorses, as we would expect from knights. But Japanese horses were smaller than our steeds, and when some English horses were taken to Japan the weight of them made it difficult for them to move through the mud and the rice paddies. However, the smaller breed of horse used by the Japanese had little trouble with the mud. When the first horses measuring 16 hands (which is quite big for a horse) came to the more rural places in Japan, the Japanese were astonished. In one case, they had to cut away a non-vital beam to fit an English horse into a Japanese stable.

The Japanese Emperor Is an English Knight

Believe it or not, but on paper Emperor Meiji of Japan (1852–1912) was an English knight, and an Italian one, and Spanish, and Swedish … you get the idea. When Japan entered the modern world, foreign powers gave him various honours, one of which is the English rank of Order of the Garter, the famous order of knights. Of course, this is just a 'paper honour' and he was not in any way a real English knight, as you would imagine. This trend continued down the line of Japanese emperors. Even to this very day, the Emperor of Japan is also a member of the Order of the Garter and of many other Western orders, making him a

knight in many countries. For all time, it will be recorded that some of the greatest orders of chivalry in the world had Japanese emperors as members.

The Emperor Who Was Struck Off the List of Knights

The Emperor Showa, who ruled during the Second World War, was actually a Knight of the Order of the Garter and a Field Marshal in the British Army by appointment. This was quite embarrassing at the start of the war, and when the Japanese entered the war these appointments were taken away from him and he was officially struck off the order of knights. This means that technically one of the British high-ranking army officers was the head of state for the enemy. The emperor's status as knight was restored in 1971 and the knight on the 'wrong' side of the war was brought back into knighthood.

The English Prince in a Japanese Chivalric Order

Chivalric orders seem to be just passed around royal families. After bestowing the Order of the Garter on the Emperor of Japan the Prince of England returned to his rooms. The emperor then appeared at the princes' rooms with a box and gave him the Order of the Chrysanthemum (Japan's highest order). Mitford says that the emperor pulled out the medallion and placed it around his neck himself, something never before done – the closest thing at the time being that the emperor once opened the box for someone – making it an outstanding honour.

Banzai!

We have all heard the famous shouts of '*Banzai, Banzai, Banzai!*' It is similar to the English 'Hurrah!' Japanese sailors did not use that term; they used '*Hoga!*' *Banzai* means 'ten thousand years', i.e. long life, but *Hoga* means 'to salute'.

For Merit

Three Japanese high-ranking military men received the Order of Merit from the King of England through the royal prince in Japan, and it was the first time it was ever given to anyone who was not British. These were given for the Japanese victory over the Russians. The Japanese found it against their culture to honour themselves by wearing the words 'for merit' outwardly, as it goes against the Japanese way of not boasting, so they turned them around to hide the words. The English had to explain that this was against etiquette and dress code, so the Japanese reluctantly turned them the correct way.

The First Toast of Japan

In 1906, when the Japanese Emperor and Prince Arthur of Britain had exchanged chivalric orders, there was a state dinner. The emperor toasted the King of England and the band played 'God Save the King'. This was the first time in history that the Emperor of Japan had given a toast and in it he wished good health to the King of England.

Guinness in Japan

By the year 1900 or so, the names of Allsopp, Bass and Guinness were household names in Japan.

Agreements are Made When Entertaining

When I published my first book in Japanese, I asked about the contract, at which they looked puzzled. It seems they did not do contacts. Now, I knew that Japanese business was done on one's word, but even in publishing not even the percentages were signed for; it was all just agreed. I had been told that Japanese business deals were made when both sides involved were at dinner, drinking and in karaoke booths, and that the details were ironed out afterwards. Of course, ironing out the details can be a long and arduous journey in Japan, but as long as the initial agreement is made, then both sides are set upon sorting out any issues. Interestingly, Mitford comments on this, saying it is strange that such national decisions should be made to the sounds of Japanese traditional music during the joy of a dinner party. Nothing much has changed since then.

Scam the Foreigner

Mitford, on his return to Japan, was enjoying the beautiful scenery, when sellers of wooden toys and boxes came to his house. After he had been looking at them for a short while, his Japanese friend Kata came to see him, and the merchants dropped their prices dramatically as they realised this was not easy target for cash.

File Your Paperwork

There was once a Japanese translator who dealt with the Dutch language. He forgot to submit a translation of an official document and was imprisoned for five years.

The Reality of European Influence

Japan maintained its Middle Ages culture for longer than most countries in the world, and the change from the old ways to the modern was drastic and fast. An interesting account comes from Mitford, who demonstrates this change by the image of European royal visits to Japan and times that he had access to the emperor:

 1869 The emperor is in full medieval court dress, accompanied by court nobles in Chinese fashion.

 1873 The emperor is now in full European uniform, riding in a Western carriage surrounded by western-style Japanese lancers.

 1906 The men around the emperor were all modelled on Western-style ministers, stars and medals at their jacket breast and noblewomen in the most up-to-date French dresses.

Behind the Red Curtain

When the shogun officially meets the Emperor of Japan, he kneels down in front of a red curtain and the emperor speaks from behind it. This is, of course, in times of peace or in times when the emperor is stable in the ancient city of Kyoto.

The Shake of Hands That Shook the Nation

Even today, it is forbidden to shake the hand of the emperor or to pass him something directly. But back in 1906 when Prince Arthur (son of Queen Victoria) came to Japan, not only did the emperor come to meet Prince Arthur from inside the confines of his palace, but he shook his hand! This was an unprecedented move and one that resounded in Japanese society as a massive confirmation of Anglo-Japanese relations.

The Good Old Days

Those people who were alive between 1850 and into the 1900s used the word *mukashi* to mean 'old times'. It came to signify a massive change for them. These people witnessed the time of the samurai in the earlier life, when street beheadings, the vicious torture and execution of criminals, and grand warlord parades were common, and life was bound up in medieval ways and in the culture of ancient China. In the second part of their life they saw a total revolution and the coming of Western laws, ways, technology and culture. To them, 'the good old days' were actually different from their today.

Otters and Revolvers

One night, Mitford was staying in the most beautiful scenic spot as a guest in a house, when he heard a clatter of clogs outside the room. His samurai friend picking up his sword and Mitford drawing his revolver, they made ready to protect themselves. But there was laughter all around when it was discovered that the noise was just two women placing a wooden cover over the pond to stop otters eating the fish.

The Development of Japanese Style

In the 1400s, the now iconic tatami floor mat started to become popular, and wealthy people began to carpet their homes with them. Also, bamboo blinds were being replaced by the now universal paper sliding door. Things that were relatively more complex were simplified, and the style known as *wabi* – rustic and simple – became the vogue after the love of all things Chinese started to become outdated.

The Replacement of Men of Pedigree With Men of Talent

Mitford states that as he saw the movement of Japan from its last feudal times to the new age, men in position due to their pedigree and family gave way to men of talent, and that talent now opened doors that before were closed. This does not mean that Japan left the old families behind. In fact, many old and powerful families used their wealth to get into business and position, but it did mean that the once 'boys club only' approach started to break down and new blood came in.

The True Meaning of *Geisha*

We all know the word *geisha*, meaning a lady with white skin, gorgeous hair and a fan who dances for guests at a party. However, the word *geisha* actually has the meaning of a person who is skilled in the arts, 'art-person'. So actually in medieval Japan, a *geisha* was most likely someone who performed one of the arts and the *geisha* you are thinking of was most likely called *geiko*. Now the name *geisha* no longer means any person of the arts, but has come to mean only those women in Kyoto.

The Cycle of Talent Over Pedigree

There are two elements you should be aware of when thinking of samurai lineages and position within Japanese society. People often think that only those born into a samurai family are in fact samurai and that only people of certain families and birth can advance. The actual case is that this goes in cycles. Part one is a rise of the talented, people of ability who take on power by their own devotion to a goal. Next comes the period of tradition, where descendants of men of ability form a 'boys club', and birth and connection open doors. However, after this comes decline, and men of talent are again called upon to take up positions so that tasks can be done. This is perhaps the same across the whole of human society, but the lesson here is to not forget this cycle in relation to Japan. This is true from the rise of the first great samurai families to the upheaval of the Sengoku Period, when lower samurai turned society on its head, all the way to the Meji Restoration, when fighters were hired from the lower classes. It is not always the case that once a samurai, always a samurai, or that if born low, a person remains low.

The Merchant's Pleasure

There is rich and then there is *rich*. Here is an example of some of the profit that some merchants could make by trading with China.

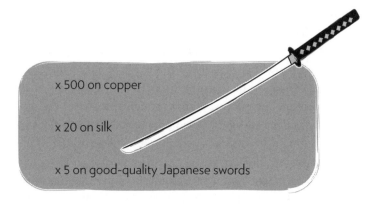

x 500 on copper

x 20 on silk

x 5 on good-quality Japanese swords

To not create confusion, let us talk in units instead of currency. One merchant received 25,000 units of profit for his work; in Japan it took 10,000 units of the same currency to build a palace. Therefore, that year, that merchant could have built two and a half palaces. This puts the rise of the merchant class in wealth over the increasingly poor samurai into context. Samurai had the prestige and the power, but merchants had the cash. It was recorded that some ships could carry up to 100 tonnes of cargo and many smaller craft were travelling between Japan and the mainland. Chinese ships were considered to be the best until the Portuguese arrived with Western technology in the 1500s.

The Medici of the East

Like the famous Florentine banking family, some Japanese families created a moneylending and banking system. They based their trade on speculation, investment and interest. The rise of this new type of business gave massive revenues to the military government when they started taxing this newfound and mysterious income that was based on nothing but an idea.

The Sake Industry

Some sake merchants rivalled warlords for their wealth; the income from these vast business empires outdid the money gained from the land. Remember, in later days, the samurai had their honour but the merchants had the cash.

The Birth of Okinawa

We often think of Japan as a 'closed' country, but China did it first. During the Ming Dynasty, China closed its borders and restricted movement. This left a void in the trade network that was filled by the Japanese, the Malays and the Koreans. This had the after-effect of giving birth to Okinawa. Okinawa has had influences from many places because of its geographic position. But this burst in trade made it a centre of commerce in that area and it became a melting pot of Asian culture, giving it uniqueness to this day.

The Hybrid Language

In the 1800s, the port of Yokohama was a centre of foreign influence, and a strange hybrid language of Japanese, Dutch, Malay and English developed where people could talk in each other's languages in 'pigeon form'.

The Cambridge and Oxford Society of Japan

Around the year 1900, Japanese people who had attended Oxford and Cambridge universities were returning to Japan from England. In 1903, the Cambridge Society was formed, but it then amalgamated into the Cambridge and Oxford Society in 1905 (much to the displeasure of Oxford at coming second in the name). To this day, the society meets, and Japanese graduates of both universities return to Japan and join the society. More information can be found about them online.

The Japanese Union

In Japan, an early form of union was created, known as an *ikki*. This was be a collection of villages, bands, common people or warriors who stuck together to protect themselves. They ensured the following three points:

- To repel invaders and over-ambitious governers

- To act as peacekeepers, to provide a form of social service and help those in need within the community

- To suppress civilian unrest

The Five Mountains of Zen

In the Song Dynasty China there were five temples on five mountains that were prominent and important: this was known as the five-mountain system. This arrangement of religious structure came to Japan, but they had over 230 temples in their five-temple system.

A New Jerusalem

After the Onin War in the 1400s, Kyoto became a cultural melting pot and moved away from its very court-style existence. Many new levels of society came to mix there and culture took on a new breath of life.

Legends About the Emperor

When researching the journals of Western people in Japan, and the ample academic articles discussing them, the question of the records pertaining to the Japanese Emperor always came up. From the first Catholic priests in Japan before the end of samurai times, speculation about the emperor was rife. The problem is that very few people ever got to see the imperial person, and it was only at the time of Mitford that the emperor started to show himself to the world. Therefore, the following list is a record of what was said about the emperor from those on the outside, not those on the inside, so there may be more legend than fact. The jury is still out on the actual truth:

He has to sit on a throne like a statue all day, solemnly, as he represents Japan and Japan must be in a state of calm.

He has to wear a heavy crown.

He uses only plain and brand-new pots to eat and drink from, after which they are broken so that no one else can use them.

If someone else does use them, he will become drastically ill.

His nails and hair are left to grow naturally.

No knife may touch him.

A woman bites off his hair (and nails?).

No sun or direct moonlight may touch him.

No one outside the palace may look at him; when he travels, paper shutters are placed over all windows.

Attendants clean his hands after he touches anything (which leads to these attendants having very rough hands and complaining about it; also their feet, which must be bare).

CHILDREN OF THE SUN

A 1300s document was used in twentieth-century Japanese classrooms and was frequently quoted to 'prove' that Japan was indeed the land of real gods, that the very soil of Japan was divine and to die for Japan was the path of heaven.

Samurai Honour in a New Age

Mitford says that the new world of Japan of the early twentieth century still maintained the honour of the samurai, but instead of crying out loud 'my life for my lord', the new cry was 'my life for the Emperor'.

The Fall of Decent Society

In the year 1334, an anonymous writer said that the following negative elements had entered the society of the capital city:

- Night raids
- Robbery
- False documents
- False nobles
- False lineages
- Easy women
- Fast horses in the street
- Misguided monks
- Slander
- Low-quality hawks
- Poor-quality swords
- Emaciated horses
- Old and battered armour
- The renting of armour
- Indulging in base sports

Temple Pimps

There were some Buddhist temples that would offer protection for prostitutes as long as they got a cut of their takings.

The Outcastes

Some readers may have heard of Japan's outcastes, those who were not from the samurai, farmer, artisan and merchant tiers of the system. Their role was to deal with the lesser tasks that others did not want to undertake, such as the disposal of corpses, both human and livestock, the cleaning away of filth, and all the menial tasks you can think of. These outcastes are known to have been persecuted right up until the twentieth century, and the problem has only recently disappeared from modern Japan. However, in Japanese history they appear to have been much more integrated in society and an accepted part of it; some of them ran inns, cleaning services and other tasks, and were accepted among the general population. These people are what are known as 'marginalised' – those who live on the 'outskirts' of a society. These people often also existed physically near rivers and in places not so desirable to others. When imagining old Japan, think of shanty towns at the river's edge and of those semi-outcaste members of society who later became persecuted. They even performed executions for the lord of the area.

The Merger of the Classes

Samurai life had continued for 1,000 years, for the last 250 years of which the samurai had been a class in almost total lockdown, under the governance of a single family. Thus the merging of all classes of society, in the second half of the 1800s, was a difficult affair. At the top were princes and lords of great realms, below them the samurai, below them the commoners and below them the outcastes. When the class system broke down, there was technically no real divide between the people, apart from the recognition of a noble class, and it was said that only a newly appointed position in the new government regime meant distinction from others. However, this was not true. If a man was an ex-lord of a domain, he was still known as a grand prince, and the ex-samurai had their new title of *shizoku* (warrior family) but, on a darker side, some men would not eat next to the outcaste class. Even so, the merger of the classes was quite speedy, and it is recorded that in one military academy there were nobles, ex-samurai, commoners and ex-outcastes all working together. Of course, powerful families took powerful roles, but the class divide had broken.

A School in Western Medicine

In Japanese the word *ryu* means school, lineage or tradition. So, for example, the school I practise personally is Natori-Ryu, the warfare school of the Natori family. Also, in martial arts circles you will hear the word *ko-ryu*, which means old schools, that is, schools which were established in samurai times. The word *ryu* is laden with old samurai prestige. However, there were actually *ko-ryu* based on Western medicine, meaning that if a samurai studied these schools they could get a *Menkyo Kaden* (full licence) in the arts of Western medicine from a samurai school! (And I do not often use exclamation points!)

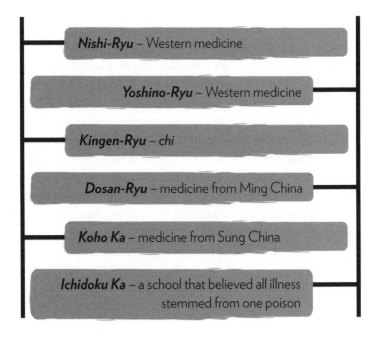

- **Nishi-Ryu** – Western medicine
- **Yoshino-Ryu** – Western medicine
- **Kingen-Ryu** – chi
- **Dosan-Ryu** – medicine from Ming China
- **Koho Ka** – medicine from Sung China
- **Ichidoku Ka** – a school that believed all illness stemmed from one poison

The above schools and movements (those ending in *ka*) were in contest for popularity in Japan. Before the 1600s, there was very much a slant towards China-based ideas. When with the Jesuits came Western concepts, the Dutch brought medicine, and by the end of the 1800s the old ways of China, *chi* and herbs, were giving way to science and Western schools. If anyone asks you what samurai *ko-ryu* you study, tell them it is *Nishi-Ryu*, the way of Western medicine.

The Village People

The idea of the quaint Japanese village with blacksmith, fishmonger, potter, etc. may be a slightly fantasised idea. It is actually quite possible that before the age of wars, most people outside of great cities actually lived in small hamlets and farm collectives. Then, most people would have been attached to a farm which was positioned within its own borders, and people came together at festivals when the different clans and farm populations met to watch theatre, exchange goods or celebrate together. Village life as the normal might not have been the case in early Japan and it might be that smaller communities thrived and produced certain things, or that they were mostly self-sufficient with minimal trade. The landscape of Japan might have been one of hamlets within the wide hills and open plains of Japan, and later on populations were forced into dense villages and then into an ever-growing number of cities.

People of the Sea

While many people lived in hamlets or the great cities, there was a group of people known as the 'sea people', aquatic experts and dwellers along the shore. They were semi-nomadic and moved in fleets of boats along coasts, shorelines, rivers and lakes, setting up habitation in the fields around these areas to stock up provisions and commodities, such as salt and fish, and then moving on to other places. These bronze-bodied sailors and their fleet were a community on the waves who sailed out of history.

To Write in English Letters

One of the concerns of Anglo-Japanese relations was the attempt to establish the Japanese script into what is known in Japanese as *romaji* – the English alphabet. Of course, in the late 1800s and early 1900s the Japanese people as a whole were new to this style. There was even a discussion about publishing Japanese books in English letters, but this just did not work for the Japanese. Today, as ever, the Japanese read in their own alphabet and, while you can see English letters all over Japan, books remain the domain of Japanese characters, and the English script never caught on in Japan for literature.

Men of the Land

At times, in Japan, it was the case that a samurai who had won land by war was permanently connected to that land and could not be removed from it by legal process; they had paid in blood to acquire it and it was only by war that it could be taken. Therefore, there was a trend of false accusations and attempts at land grabbing, and a 'legal' use of force would be used to 'rightfully' dispossess the samurai of their land by war. The lack of space and want for power led to many skirmishes, with samurai trying to increase their holdings in a less than chivalric way.

Japanese Theatre

There are multiple forms of Japanese theatre, but there are three main types that are popular:

No – a sombre, minimalist and high-cultured theatre
Kabuki – loud, dramatic and colourful theatre
Bunraku – puppet theatre on stage

Hide Your Face

The showing of emotion in Japan is deemed something that should not be done, and, therefore, often the Japanese cover their faces. This was more prominent in old Japan, where the whole sleeve of a kimono could be used or the entirety of an open fan. This even extended to the use of masks when audience members attended plays and theatre, giving us the strange and weird idea of masked people in a theatre audience.

Indian Culture in Japan

One large element of Japanese and samurai society that is sometimes not recognised is Indian culture, which is very much part of Japanese life. Buddhism may have come through the filter of mainland Asia but it is, in essence, an Indian subject. The Buddha, Buddhism and some other elements have their origins in India. Many of the sutras studied in Japan were written in India, the magic spells and chants, including those in Sanskrit, come from India, and many of the saints venerated are Indian.

Buddha Becomes a God

Buddha was, of course, a human, and his words a philosophy, but he and his words eventually acquired a divine status and a faith-based system developed.

Chinese Monks in Japan

In short, China was 'cool' and all things Chinese were considered to be great by the Japanese for a long time. Therefore, Chinese monks in Japan held status, and some Chinese monks did, in fact, settle in Japan to teach. Hundreds of monks eventually came to Japan and taught many aspects of Buddhism, including Zen, the famous *sumi-e* ink painting style, Chinese poetry, Confucianist writings and estate management. Japanese monks also travelled to China to study there under Chinese masters.

Rape

It is difficult to establish just how serious the Japanese law courts took rape. In certain situations, rape carried the death penalty, but in others it was considered a light affair. *Natori-Ryu* war manuals from the 1600s state that any soldier in a siege who raped another's wife would be put to death, or that if soldiers captured and raped enemy women, they too would be killed, but in truth this was more about military discipline. In times of peace, the punishment for raping a woman walking alone was for the man to have his head half shaven to make him stand out, and would have to wear it like this until it grew out, identifying him as a rapist.

Do Not Shout at the Judge

The last thing you should do in a medieval Japanese court was shout at the judge. Shouting at the judge was an automatic guilty verdict and many 'crimes' carried the punishment of death.

Court Adjourned

Getting a lawsuit through a medieval Japanese court could be problematic. Courts would not go into session on inauspicious and unlucky days according to the old Chinese calendar. If someone connected to the court died they would adjourn for fifty days, and if someone was ill they would also postpone the case.

The Population of Japan

The estimated population of Japan in the 1100s was approximately 7 million people, while the population of New York in 2016 was approximately 8.5 million. Therefore, the great age of chivalric Japan played out with roughly the same amount of people as modern-day New York.

Drums and Fields

The planting of rice and other crops was often accompanied by singing and rhythm, including drummers at the sides of paddies drumming a beat. The drummers could be children, and the entire planting process followed a tempo that allowed the work to flow.

SOCIAL CONSTRUCTION OF JAPAN

Kuni – The country

Kokka – A country

IE – A clan

The Importance of Rice

Never underestimate the importance of rice in Japan; it was the foundation of their society. When rice production was down, some states had to buy rice in from other states, or some areas that had continually low production of rice would have a higher production of other commodities.

However, this meant that in times of war, certain states could starve out others and famine would quickly follow. Rice was the foundation of all Japan.

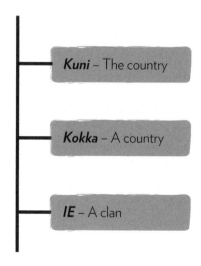

Fish is Not the Diet of the Japanese

We often assume that fish is the staple diet of the Japanese, and in modern Japan it is. However, in older days, certain landlocked states that were not on the coast would have to trade to buy fish in, which is not a problem in times of peace, but in war the trade routes stop or cannot function. This means that the idea of the Japanese enjoying lots of fish is only true in times of peace or along the coast. People in other places, with less access to water locally, had to eat other foods, making fish cheap in some areas and expensive in others at certain times. The idea of a unified trade system that delivers fish all over Japan in a never-ending sushi conveyer belt is a modern one.

What is the Land Worth?

An important aspect to remember is that the value of land in old Japan is not quite the same as our idea of the value of land. Most people buy a house and wait for its value to increase, selling at a profit and moving up the property ladder. However, in Japan, houses could be pulled down and reconstructed, like a jigsaw, so the value was not always in the house itself, but in the production of the land. The value of the farm production per annum was the important aspect – in essence, what the land could produce. This means that when houses have to be moved, or land changes hands, the loss or gain is calculated from the annual production of the farm and is not from the selling and acquiring of the house or buildings. While they do hold value, of course, often our idea of the value of buildings confuses our understanding of the value of the land.

When Did the Sengoku Period End?

In the history of Japan, you will come across references to the Sengoku Period, which translates to The Warring States Period. However, the date of its end is often changed from author to author. The period itself was a time when the lesser samurai houses turned society on its head and ousted the old rule and brought in a new one, the time of the upside-down movement. However, it created over 100 years of war, until the country started to settle again. This age of wars started in the second half of the 1400s. However, the end of the warring period is considered to be when this upheaval ended amd some people date that to 1570 and the rise of the warlord Hideyoshi, who took control of whole country by the 1580, but others fix it at 1600 with the Battle of Seigahara. Others still place it at 1603, when the victorious Tokugawa Ieyasu was declared shogun of all Japan. Therefore, from book to book the date varies.

Interest in the West

In the first half of the 1700s, the shogun known as Tokugawa Yoshimune had the Dutch traders ride horses around an arena, shooting pistols and controlling the horses, but because they said that they were not trained in such matters he ordered them to send someone with training on their next trip. That person was Jurgen Keijser, but he was poisoned and robbed during his stay in Japan. In fact, it was not until 1725 that Western horse breeds started to properly arrive in Japan, but even so they did not become popular until much later. The shogun also had the Dutch display how to wear Western armour in the correct manner, and ordered a suit of armour that could withstand bullets. It was not until 1732 that the armour was given, and there were a few problems along the way. In addition to this, the shogun asked them to demonstrate many Western things, such as eating at a table, using a knife and fork, table set-up and many other daily activities from the West. It is said the shogun observed these things but did not partake, but he did order many things from the West, including food, cutlery, tables, beds, cloth and various animals. At this point Japan was indeed a closed country, but through the small hold the Dutch had, Western tradition leaked into Japan and started to build up, gaining acceptance until the ships of the famous sea master Commodore Perry set changes in motion, opening Japan again to the world.

Book Burning

During the height of the anti-Christian era in Japanese history, the government had bouts of burning Western books that contained any reference to religion.

The Diet of Monks

It is well known that Buddhist monks observe a strict diet, eat frugally and abstain from vices. Well, actually no, that's not true. Many chroniclers tell of Japanese monks' outward appearances, value of virtue, strict eating habits and the like. However, behind closed doors, they ate what they pleased, dealt in money, sodomised boys and dealt with prostitutes. It could be said that these are evil attacks from the clergy on Japanese religion, but in truth, it seems a large number of Japanese religious figures only put on an outward appearance of Buddhist law. Myself, I have seen golf-playing monks, the drinking of copious amounts of alcohol, the owning of sports cars, Harley Davidson motorbikes, vast quantities of food eaten and my all-time favourite, a *yamabushi* mountain hermit on a train listening to music through earphones, alighting from the train, and having a smoke.

Women's Rights

In all of these accounts it appears that women had a bad hand in life, and that they were secluded and controlled. But often the texts differ. As stated in the introduction, this is actually because of different attitudes and situations at different times. However, one account by Jorge Alvares states that the woman were respected by their husbands and 'often rule their menfolk'. Also, if divorced, woman could regain their land that was given in dowry and some could even take a level of control over estate affairs. Just remember that in medieval society not all people were equal, some women had freedom, some were married and hidden away, some were sold into prostitution, some became powerful, some were warriors, etc. As Japan went through different periods of social change, so did the rights of both men and women, and men were, at times, equally controlled by society.

Time of the Month

Women in the menstrual cycle removed themselves from any work and had a week of leisure to deal with the pain; maidservants and the like simply stayed away. This seclusion was mainly done in small huts set aside for the purpose. The reason for this was that blood was considered unclean in certain aspects.

Had a Baby, Have You?

One strange account tells that women, after giving birth, stayed in a single room for one month with no one to talk to and no interaction. They were simply passed food and water and went to the toilet when needed.

Lawsuits

A Japanese person could not bring a lawsuit against their parents, and nor could a vassal bring a lawsuit against their master.

The New and Old

Western plays are normally written anew, with new stories and new ideas, each playwright aiming to create something fresh. In Japan, they stick to old plays and ones that are known by and familiar to audiences.

THE JAPANESE FAN

The Japanese used to almost always carry a fan, they used these to write messages on lest they forget important information, or they held exquisite ones with scenes of old or famous ideas. They also had poems and sayings of great masters on them. It was very rude to fan yourself in front of someone superior and larger fans were used by pageboys while guests ate.

Japanese Names

It is well known that Japanese names are given in the order of family first and then their given names, like my favourite samurai, Natori Masazumi, which would be the same as saying Cummins Antony. The Western chronicler Francois Caron claims that the Japanese told him that the names of the family go first because it is the name of their parents and that their parents are most important and, in this way of naming, the family and their ancestors are honoured. The given name may be changed multiple times throughout a person's life.

There Be Gold

The Japanese way of panning for gold involves establishing that gold is indeed in a river, after which they will direct the river in a new direction. The old river dries up and then they dig out the bed and sift through the ground to find the grains of gold that have fallen to the riverbed because of their weight.

Rowing

The Japanese did not row a boat like us. They sat back to back, facing out to sea on either side of the boat, and they used a form of sculling motion in the water without bringing their oars out of the water. They did this while singing sea shanties.

Becoming 3 Years Old in Only One Year and a Few Days

In Japan, the number zero did not exist, only the concept of nothing. Therefore, if someone was born they could not be nothing, and there was no such thing as the number zero. This meant that a baby was 1 year old on the day it was born, and the ages of all people went up at New Year. This meant that a baby born just before New Year was 2 years old when only a few days old and after one year, at the next New Year, they became 3 years old. This meant that a baby who was actually only 1 year and three or four days old was counted as a 3-year-old in old Japan.

The Strange Case of Shoe Removal

It is well known that Japanese people remove their shoes before entering a house. However, chronicle after chronicle refers to the Japanese removing their shoes in the street when they met someone they deemed important. A person of lesser standing, when addressing a person of higher standing, removed their sandals and either held them in hand, or stood on the edge of them, having removed the toes from the straps at the front. Japanese sources state that wearing the common Japanese-style straw sandal was also considered rude when visiting someone of higher station.

SCHOOL'S OUT

Children who were educated were
done so by monks in old Japan, but
the children of the wealthy had home
teachers to school them

Drawing a Weapon Can Get You Killed

In certain circumstances, the drawing of a weapon in anger and
in the incorrect place could get you the death penalty. Remember
the famous case of the forty-seven *ronin* who took revenge for
their lord. The lord drew his weapon and attempt to injure
another in anger, and as a result had to commit suicide. Such was
the strictness of Japanese law at times.

Night Soil

Night soil is the polite word given to human excrement. A household would sell their human waste or exchange it for rice, as it
was collected by gong farmers (people who used to collect and
sell human waste from each house). These men took the waste
and sold it on as fertiliser, making it a lucrative business.

MILESTONES

Across Japan, markers were set up to
show the distance travelled, similar to
milestones, but these were mounds.
If one needed to be positioned exactly
where someone had built their house,
the house was pulled down and
moved to a different location.

The Horns of Dread

In one less-trusted account, where fact is not assured but not
totally absent, it states that in one city, each house should have a
horn (probably a conch shell) and that in an emergency all should
blow their horns so that the population of the city can be warned.

The number of blows on the horn and their meanings were:

1 = Tumult

2 = Fire

3 = Robbery

4 = Treason

The Act of Fake Retirement

There is a custom in Japan known as *inkyo*, which is a form of fake retirement. People in political positions will often retire well before their time. Both the Shogun and the Emperor of Japan actually retire and do not pass on succession through death as in Western society. A leader can stand down so that their successor can take over political control without a battle from competing leaders after the death of a central figure. This ensures dynastic stability and allows for little contest of succession. Each leader appoints their heir and passes the mantle on while still alive, and in this way no one can lie about the previous leader's intent and succession can flow. However, often power may not have been passed on with succession, and power may continue to be in the hands of the retired leader or a council of men, as was the case with the emperor.

The Beauty and Modernity of Kyoto

Kyoto may be an ancient city, but even in ancient times it was modern in many aspects. The streets were swept twice a day and washed down, each and every resident and shop owner being responsible for their own part of the street outside of their shops and houses, which were to be kept clean. Each shop and house had its own crest telling customers what was for sale and which family owned it, and parts of the city had arcades, that people could walk along, which kept off the rain and sun. Commerce was busy at times and the whole city had the feel of a modern commercial metropolis built on the ancient customs of the emperor and religious centres.

The Tea Ceremony

The following account of a Japanese tea ceremony is from João Rodrigues' experiences in the 1590s and written down in 1604. The tea ceremony has undergone certain changes from then until now.

A tea house should be in the same compound or area as the house of the owner, but the entrance gate would be different from the main gateway. The pathway would be of stepping stones and a standing rock basin would offer a place to wash, unless it was bitter cold, and in such a case warm water would be waiting inside. The entrance to the actual tea house would have been small and had benches to the side so that the guest could wait while preparations were being made. Nearby was a toilet, scrupulously clean and seldom, if ever, used, more of a polite ornamented necessity than a privy for actual use, unless needs absolutely required. If such a situation arose, it was cleaned immediately. There would be a closable cupboard where fans and swords could be kept, and hats made of bark would be available to keep off any rain if they wished to go outside the tea house. The host would invite the guests inside, into the tea house itself – which was very small – and the guest had to stoop through a very low doorway. On the inside the room was lit by small windows and was adorned with a seasonal display and scroll. All talk was quiet and when the host felt that the guest had viewed enough they would sit by the stove, which was a neat place lined with fine ash and had burning charcoal to heat the water. The host would place a small table in front of each guest; the guests would lift the table to head height and bow, placing it back on the floor. The host would then place wine and rice on the table for the guests to enjoy. After the guests had finished it would be time to drink tea. At this point, the guests were asked to leave the tea house; they did so and washed their hands again and, while they were doing this, the seasonal display would be changed to represent a different season and the place would be swept. When the host was ready, he would ring a small bell to inform the guests to re-enter. The guests performed the same entrance ritual of observing the display and offering compliments. At this point, the tea ceremony was performed and tea was drunk. After this was finished, the guests left and awaited the host outside. At this point, they might retire to the house and sit in a reception room, where they might talk informally and where the appreciation of various family antiques took place. After their farewells, the guest would write to the host thanking them for their excellent hosting skills.

Before the Tea Ceremony

We think of the Japanese tea ceremony as being, well, Japanese. But originally the tea ceremony in Japan was very much a Chinese affair, with Chinese chairs, tea cabinets and was done without the now-famous accompanying flower arrangements. It was only later that Japanese tea ceremonies began to take on a more Japanese form.

Tea as Equals

In old Japan, it was acceptable for someone of lower status to invite someone of higher status to engage in a tea ceremony at their house. The lower-ranking person would invite the senior into their house and tea room to enjoy conversation and the appreciation of tea. The result of this is that they would treat each other as equals in this situation, and conversation could move freely, and perhaps any needed business could be done.

Single-Use Chopsticks

The idea of disposable chopsticks is considered a new one. However, in old Japan people of high rank used freshly carved chopsticks for each meal and never used them again. On the reverse side of this, in Japan people might have their favourite chopsticks for years and keep them in a special case. When

Western people first entered Japan they marvelled at how the Japanese never touched their food with their hands at the table and even the cooks barely touched it, instead moving it about with implements. In contrast, Europeans ate with their hands and wiped them on stained handkerchiefs, to the utter disgust of the Japanese.

Japanese Baths

Even back in the early 1600s, Japanese baths were as we see them today, scrupulously clean, fitted with dressing areas and hanging bath robes. In addition, they even had perfume pans which allowed people standing by to give their body a beautiful aroma by wafting in the perfume.

The Top Shelf

Up until recent years, 'light' and 'heavy' pornography was quite the norm in Japan, and in quite ordinary and customer-filled shops pornography was quite openly displayed and not out of reach of most people. The diplomat Henry Heusken, in the 1800s, also wrote about the openness in which parts of sexual life were displayed and that facemasks with either male genitalia for the nose, or female genitalia, were on display for all to see and buy. During my time living in Japan throughout the 2000s, there has been an extremely rapid decline in public shows of pornography. At one point this was open and brash, from prostitutes openly approaching men at train stations to overtly sexual magazines being mixed in with relatively harmless topics such as cooking. The last remnants of this are a quickly disappearing element of Japanese life, and now only the occasional man reading pornography on a train can still be seen. I would say that this element of Japanese life will be dead by the time this book has had the chance to acquire that 'old book' smell.

From Father to Son

It is difficult to truly understand the level of heredity in professions in Japan. It is safe to say that many young people were stuck with the position they were born into and simply had to perform in that area, as tradition dictated that they must take on that role. Even interpreters – that is, language specialists who had dealt with the English, the Dutch, the Spanish and the Americans – were all from the same families in the area of Hirado, be they any good at languages or not.

Follow the Old Ways ... Even if They Are Wrong

An interesting point in the journal of Henry Heusken is when he was told by a samurai named Shinano that the Japanese must follow the ways of those who have gone before them, the ancestors and the ways of the gods and saints, even if a new, better and more direct way was found. However, that was a way of later Japanese life because in the turbulent times of war that lasted almost 200 years, change and progression were the name of the game, and it was only in times of peace that society truly opted for obedience to the old ways.

One Week off at New Year

The Japanese might be hard working now, and they may have almost no time off during the year due to the pressures of commerce. However, in the Edo Period, most people had seven days off to celebrate at New Year, and festival days allowed for relaxation.

Open Rebellion Against Tourists

Article 7 of the original treaty between America and Japan was concerned with travel by Americans around Japan, about which there was much debate. The government were worried that if they simply opened up the country to all Americans and gave them free passage in all lands, the people of Japan would rise up and rebel. They said there were even places that the Japanese did not go, and therefore they should start by opening just a few places to sightseeing Americans.

Japan Is Not a Closed Country

In this book, Japan has been spoken of as a closed country. However, the samurai existed for approximately 1,000 years and for the first 700 years or so the country was in open trade with many places, including the West at certain points. It was in the 1600s that it closed its borders to trade. In fact, in the 1800s, while the samurai were still in power, they opened up trade again with the West. Many people think that Japan only opened up to the world after the samurai period ended, but actually it was the samurai class that opened Japan to the world again. However, within a decade or so, the samurai proper started to decline.

Only on Official Business

When America and Japan were creating their first treaty in 1857–58, a point was raised about American officials and the freedom of travel. The Japanese insisted that the document said that American officials could travel anywhere in the country but only on 'official businesses', to which the Americans said, 'What if they wish to travel for leisure?' To this, the Japanese replied that no matter where an official went and no matter what the reason, it would always be *official*. If the official wished to see Mount Fuji, this was a business trip for the health of the official, because the health of the official was required to do business and, therefore, no matter where an official went and for all reasons, he was on official business.

All Hail Confucius

Confucianism is the study of the teachings of Confucius, the ancient Chinese sage. While his teachings have been known in Japan for a long time, in the era of peace known as the Edo Period he was given great reverence because he taught that all people should know their place in society (a good tactic for the leaders to adopt). Because of this, Confucius was held in extremely high regard. Government officials had to study his works and know them by heart and have a deep understanding of the system, and statues of the man himself were revered as those of a god.

Servants Enter From the Opposite Side

In Japan, a guest should be seated in a position of honour. Each room was designated with areas of honour, depending on the position of the cardinal directions, and servants should enter the room from the opposite side from the position of honour, entering in the direction of the guest.

The Sandal-Bearer's Shame

When a person walked out of their house, in to a shop or into any building, if they had servants (which was not uncommon), the 'sandal boy' would place their shoes in the correct position for them, carry spares and also wait for their master's return to the outdoors and ready their sandals. In addition to this, they would also carry *getta* – clogs – and an umbrella.

waranji   geta   wara-zori   tabi   ashinaka

The term *komono* means 'lesser person' and refers to one of the lower-ranking members of society. It was these people who often took up the position of sandal bearer. Other servants could have been of noble birth, such as samurai pageboys and the like. It would be undreamed of for one of these higher-ranking servants to stoop to the level of 'shoe boy' and there may even have been awkward moments when a master would have to wait for his 'shoe boy' to arrive while the rest of his servants stood around with him, disgusted at the mere idea of picking up the sandals and placing them on the ground. (In fact, these servants might even have their own 'shoe boys', such was the lowliness of this position.) A point of interest is that servants who failed in their duties would be beaten with staffs and not the backs of sword blades, as they may try to grab the blade, which might result in the loss of fingers.

The Captain of Etiquette

Houses of the noble would have a high-ranking *soshaban*, a master of ceremonies, positioned to receive guests. This was because of the high level of sophisticated etiquette in Japanese culture and to avoid causing any social embarrassments. This was a coveted position and gave people power, and various qualified retainers would take turns on a rota for such duties.

Tea on Arrival

Japanese houses of old would have a constant supply of water on the boil and freshly ground tea leaves to be served to guests. Any guests reaching the outer gate, and who might be asked to wait for an audience, or if they were stopping to drop off a gift, would be given tea to quench their thirst. Even in Japan today, if you stop for any length of time, such as getting glasses fitted, buying a mobile phone or visiting most shops where you have to sit down, you will be offered tea. To the absolute opposite of logic, if you stop at a tea house serving English-style tea, you will first be given a cup of free Japanese tea to drink, followed by the English-style tea which you ordered (and in many cases, no longer wish to drink, as you have just drunk a cup of green tea). However, the common roadside tea shop in Japan is almost a thing of the past, but you will still see tourist boards showing pictures of old Japan saying, 'There used to be a tea rest stop here long ago', a tradition that is sadly passing out of existence.

Tea From the Hands of the High

It is a great compliment to be made and served tea by someone of higher social position. If you were a guest in an old Japanese house, the master of the house might show his respect by making and serving the tea himself.

The Gift of a Sake Cup

After drinking sake with a master of a house, the master might wish for his guest to take the cup away with him as a gift and a memory of their meeting. Henry Heusken, a diplomat in Japan during the 1800s, states that he acquired a good number of such cups but that the drink known as sake was a detestable horror that tortured him all the way between his lips and his gut.

Visiting the Ill

Strangely, in old Japan, when visiting a friend who was ill, it was expected that you would not to be allowed to enter the house. Japanese houses used to have reception areas where a guard was present and one of the duties of this guard was to record all visitors in a logbook. If the master of the house was out, if they pretended to be out, or if they were ill, the porter in this gatehouse waystation would take the message and record the names of the visitors for that day, and make notes of any gifts left. This meant that when taking a gift for an ill friend, the Japanese would have known they would not be permitted entrance, but the intention of seeing the person and the gift left behind were recorded, something which would later be remarked upon by the master of the house and would be a part of the bonds that built between friends. This made the intent to visit more important than an actual bedside visit itself.

The Fall of Feng Shui

The Japanese term for feng shui is *fusui* (風水). Before the rise of Oda Nobunaga and his massive reforms of society, many people put a lot of thought into the place where they would build, taking this ancient Chinese art into consideration. But after Oda Nobunaga took control of the country, the way that people were positioned in relation to their lord differed, and instead of having their own places the migration to castle towns began, with people being housed within the limits of the city. Therefore feng shui fell out of fashion although it did not die out.

The Great Taxation

It is often the case that when imagining society of old, the peasants are seen to be overtaxed and the wealthy over-opulent. In truth, tax and its effects fluctuates. As an example of this, consider the farmer in the 1500s. They would have farmed 1,440 square yards of land (as a unit) and been taxed on this amount. However the iron ruler of Japan, Toyotomi Hideyoshi, reduced this area to 1,210 square yards but demanded the same tax amount as for the larger area. Then, in 1586, he demanded the impractical amount of 66 per cent of their crop to be given to the state. Examples of this, including the great weapon confiscations known as 'sword hunts', divided and created a larger gap between the people and the ruling class. Therefore, this idea of the starving overtaxed peasant occurred only at certain times, when the government focused on land and squeezed out all the produce and tax they could.

The Types of Taxation

- Export tax
- Special products tax
- Provincial tax
- Commercial tax
- Frontage tax
- Land rents
- House rents
- Feudal levies
- Usury profit tax
- Toll charges and tax
- Shipping tax
- Road tax
- Transportation tax
- Guild tax

Take Down the Barriers

Barriers were set up to take tax in the form of tolls and to create money, but this had a reverse effect in that it reduced the amount of trade, so it was more profitable, at points, to remove tolls to encourage trade so that the trade goods could be taxed instead.

Utter Pawn

Being a samurai could be expensive, and as the samurai got poorer they turned to pawnbrokers. They would have to pawn some of their items to find the cash to maintain the expensive life of a samurai. The lords would then raise the tax on pawnbrokers to bring money in and would then pay the samurai from those taxes, in a cycle of diminishing returns. This, of course, is a spiralling system and is one element that led to the final result of the samurai class being in poverty by the end of the samurai period.

The Three Great Eras

It can be said the age of the samurai comes in three great eras:

the era of rule by the emperor (up to around 1200)
the era of war and upheaval (1200 to 1600)
the era of the great 'peace' (1600 to 1868).

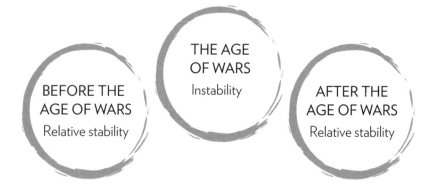

In his accounts João Rodrigues says that the first and third period were similar in that the land was under the total control of a single faction, and that many elements changed in the second period. He noted these changes:

The development of large towns and castles.
The moving of castles from fortified positions to the centre of urban areas.
The adoption of Western open-water navigation.
The widespread use of tiles on roofs in urban buildings instead of only on religious buildings.
Lasting peace made each ruler less warlike and dependent on luxury and wealth.
Ceremonies and customs went through drastic change.
Roads, sea lanes and travel became radically safer in the period of peace.
An end to pirates, privateers and bandits.
Great prosperity for the people.

Singing Prayers

Walking along the streets of old Japan, many people would carry prayer beads and chat and sing their praise of Buddha and the many deities. Each chant would mean the count of one bead until the person got all the way around the rosary and back to the start. For each bead, you should chant:

Namu Amida Butsu

After this, you should move to the next bead and chant it also, until you have got to the larger bead, denoting the start. Repeat this 10,000 times.

The Rich Get Richer

Silkworm farmers would be taxed based on the worms they owned, not the silk they sold, and therefore, sometimes they could not pay the tax bill. This meant that any small businesses would have to borrow money against future sales, which meant that many would go out of business, while the rich could fund themselves through each period and corner the market, making it easier for larger businesses and harder for smaller ones.

Trust and Money

The Japanese to this day are extremely trustworthy with money and valuables. Wallets, telephones and shopping left on a train will almost always be found in lost property at the train station. I myself heard of thieves actually returning concert tickets from a stolen bag so that the person would not miss their evening event. Shopkeepers will chase you down the street to return the smallest change and tips are seldom, if ever, given. Even back in the medieval period, the trustworthiness and honesty of the Japanese people was recorded by travellers. However, later, in the time of Mitford in the 1800s, he states quite the opposite:

> The Chinese are to me a much pleasanter people to have to deal
> with than the Japanese who are the very incarnation of treachery

... while affecting to despise trade and merchants and to respect arms and chivalry, the moment the question of money comes forward, they show an amount of greed for gain that far outdoes the much talked about cupidity of the Chinese.

Mitford, 1866

Life Without a Wife

High government officials during the Edo Period were not allowed to live with their wives. Their wives and children would remain in the capital of Edo as hostages to ensure the trust of these officials. Even the keeping of a concubine was outlawed for these gentlemen because state secrets were too important to risk pillow talk.

Bark at the Moon

In his journal, Henry Heusken states that the population of Japan were so under the rule of the shogun that all obeyed the government demand that he and the American representatives were never to be approached or spoken to. He said that all fled from the sight of the Americans, and that the group were followed by spies (*metsuke*) and guards were with them at every opportunity. He also states that so strict was the zero-approach policy that 'even dogs that had grown so old that they now only ever barked at the moon, attacked the Americans with vicious verbal warnings, not allowing them to approach'. Young women fled from them and doors and windows were closed. It was only later when the situation was relaxed that the diplomats began to talk to the locals.

Worth the Weight of Gold

In the Edo Period, the government owned all of the mines, and gold and silver had no value until the official mint struck them as coins, and any foreign coins would only have value when they were melted down and re-minted as official Japanese currency. At the end of trade negotiations with the government, and with some help from the Russians, the Americans changed the mind of the Japanese government on this point and gold and silver were measured equally (with a 'minting' tax added).

Coins, Coins, Coins

Old Japan had multiple tax systems throughout its history, and at one point the government moved from rice tax to coin tax and demanded only very high-quality coins. As a result, there was a coin shortage in the nation and all the decent coins ended up with the government.

COIN DEBASEMENT

Coin debasement means to add lower-grade metal to coins so that they keep their face value but their actual worth is less. This creates a drop in the trade value of the coin and the prices can go up. Also, in old societies, coins would be 'clipped' which means that small sections were cut off to pay for lesser items, as it was the metal that had value, not the coin.

The Quick Diplomat

There was once a case when an American diplomat wished to hand-deliver a letter to the shogun, but could not because of Japanese protocol, and this is the story of the farcical debate that followed. In 1857, a letter was presented from the United States to the Shogun of Japan, but the diplomat was not allowed to be in the presence of the ruler, and because of this an extended argument between the American and Japanese representatives ensued. At a later point in this ongoing argument, the Japanese wished to hand a letter to one of the higher-ranking diplomats, but because of illness the diplomat could not attend, and the Americans said they would pass it on to him when he was well. To which the Japanese said it was impolite to have the letter handed to someone it was not addressed to, and thus to not be allowed to hand it to the diplomat in person was dishonourable and against Japanese etiquette. To this, the Americans reminded them of their own earlier letter and the Japanese refusal to allow him to pass it to the correct authority in person, which was surely the same point, and that not allowing them to pass their letter to the shogun was then considered to be against Japan's own customs. At this point, the Japanese became confused and they had to scuttle off to find an answer to their obvious problem. Returning, the debate raged on about the correct protocol and if there were any precedents for an ambassador who had been introduced directly to the shogun, and after much debate and fuss the Japanese council said that if this was not sorted, the next time they met 'would not be under pleasant circumstances'. The Americans took this as a threat of violence, but it was, in fact, an idiom used by the Japanese to mean that if this matter was not resolved then they would have to commit suicide, which of course created more problems. After much more debate and threats of suicide, an audience with the shogun was finally given. Upon arrival in Edo, they then further attended to the issues of protocol and detail, such as who would take which position on their entrance to the castle and who would walk (because the closer you get to the centre of the castle in a palanquin the higher the rank). Finally, they came to issue of shoes indoors, because diplomats did not wish to walk in full dress without their dress shoes. The Japanese allowed the American diplomats to wear unused shoes indoors so that they did not have to go shoeless, and they walked with fresh shoes inside the shogun's residence where all the Japanese could not.

Kneel Down, Kneel Down!

In old days gone by, walking on the roads of Japan one might hear the words, '*shita ni iro, shita ni iro*' 'kneel down, kneel down!', at which the common folk would move to the sides of the roads and kneel down, hands in front of them, bowing in respect as a great prince or envoy passed through the area. However, it seems that the people of Edo (Tokyo) actually ignored this order in a distaining way, in a manner somewhat reminiscent of all city folk who ignore all around them. The same command was given when a gift from the Shogun of Japan was sent to people in other places; as the gift moved along, people were asked to kneel in front of it.

The More Powerful You Are, the Less You Are Seen

In old Japan, the more popular or powerful you were, the more you hid yourself from the eyes of the people. Common folk walked in the open, higher ranks were carried in palanquins, but the higher a person ascended the less they were seen by the masses. To be seen was to be lower, so great processions were spectacles where people did not see the famous people, but saw their closed carriage.

Spies, Spies, Spies!

Western travellers in old Japan often talked about the spies of Japan. They were referring to the internal spies who watched everything. They were placed at important events, they watched the districts, and they observed all different levels of society. These were *metsuke*, a form of internal observer. It is obvious from the collected literature that the Edo government had a series of networks that observed both their own people and any guests to the country. Some were open and admitted that they were inspectors, checking the 'welfare' of the country; others followed people at a distance. An interesting episode comes from one traveller who said that even though almost everybody was polite in Japan, some Japanese were prone to take a haughty stance towards him, but in a shock turn of events, when he was alone with that person, they would deeply apologise and say they had to behave in such a way because the place was covered in spies and that they could only let their guard down when they were alone.

Laws Above Moral Principle

Sometimes the law can become contrived and work against common sense or moral principle. There is even a phrase for this in Japan:

Ri wo yaburu ho
[Laws that override moral principle]

One document that deals with local law, called the *Jinkaishu*, says the following:

Wounding with a sword is forbidden and furthermore, anyone so wounded by a sword should not take up an act of revenge but should instead wait for the judgement of the court, even though the way of revenge is a basic principle of the samurai.

Even the samurai at times were asked to not carry out the way of the samurai and to replace their moral principles with overall laws.

The Japanese Magna Carta

Magna Carta is an English legal document that states the foundations of individual freedom and a restraint on the powers of the King of England. In Japan, each warlord would write his own law code system, which he would hope would last generations and, surprisingly, the lords at times even wrote laws that protected their subjects from them and any future lords, giving rights to the people and restrictions to the lords. One rule was that a retainer could be sentenced without a fair hearing and trial.

Evil Bands

The 1300s saw the rise of a particular warrior-bandit known as *akuto*. It is recorded that they wore yellow face scarfs and dressed in part in female clothes and carried rusty swords. The use of yellow was a mark of the outcaste class and the strange, and they used the image of the mysterious *yamabushi* mountain dwellers in a hope to instil fear. These bandits targeted coin collection points such as rents, tax and tolls, and terrorised the landscape of Japan during this period. However, we have to be careful, as in some records one side may claim that other samurai were not actual warriors but these feared bandits, in an attempt to slander them, so a distinction must be made between the real ones and those labelled as them.

Indian-Style Street Sellers

We all know the popular image of street sellers in India, women in colourful outfits sitting on cushions at the side of the road selling wondrous things. Well, Japan was the same; women sat at the sides of the street in Japanese cities and sold their wares from mats.

Japanese Polo

There is a game called *dakyu*, which is a Japanese form of polo. Two mounted teams use small nets on sticks to pick up a ball and score points. This is over 1,000 years old and went through differing stages of popularity. It was used to train military riders and was played in traditional Japanese costume.

The Calamity of the Dancing Horse

In Japan, a great fire is known as 'the calamity of the dancing horse'; this is based on a Chinese classic. In Sung China there was a tower called the Tower of the Dancing Horse, which burnt down. Because of the Japanese love for Chinese classics, they adopted this term to mean a great fire.

Architecture

Train Stations Were Once Meeting Points

If you have been to Japan you may have been to stations such as Shinjuku and Harajuku. The word *juku* derives from a form of meeting place or traveller's stop, and these have turned into larger cities now.

The Lights Have Gone Out

Any traveller to Japan will tell you of the great stone and iron lanterns that line the avenues up to temples, these are called *toro*. Unfortunately, these lamps are no longer lit. In old times those people who donated the lanterns would have their name upon them and an annual donation was given to maintain the lights at night. This means that once upon a time these lanterns would have burnt across Japan, but this custom has fallen out of favour now and the lights have died out.

The Glory of Tokyo

The gorgeous city of Edo, modern-day Tokyo, according to travellers, was a sight to behold, each district having its own guild and theme, such as a street of silver workers, a street of carpenters, a street of blacksmiths, an area for prostitutes, etc. The streets were extremely clean (as they are today) and a person could hire a horse at different way stations. The people busied themselves, and the city was alive. The richer people, and those of privilege, lived in separate parts of the city and many had their family crests painted above their house gateways in splendid fashion.

The Two-Stage House-Warming Party

When a new house was built, the neighbours would send gifts to the house and many would attend a very quiet ceremony in front of one of the main pillars, where the gifts would be viewed and all in attendance would act properly. Then they would crack open the booze and get somewhat 'legless' and have fun. However, it is often said that the Japanese do not get too drunk for fear of insulting another, which can turn nasty indeed.

Kneel Before Guests

In earlier Japan, the gap between the earth floor – where people take off their shoes – and the wooden platform and entrance to a house used to be higher. When a guest arrives at the door, it is proper manners to kneel down and talk to them, but this is an old way, and modern Japanese houses only have a very small step nowadays. However, I often stay at Eunji Temple in Wakayama, and whenever a guest rings at the door the Yamamoto family kneel down to bid them welcome or farewell. Often Japanese people look at me strangely when I do the same at the temple, as it is rare to see a Western person follow such old ways. Imagine the old days, when people would kneel as you came in and kneel as you went out.

ANT PREVENTION

Small basins filled with water are placed at the bottom of cupboard legs so that ants will not crawl over and climb up into the cupboard.

A Quick Erection

Francesco Carletti states that an average Japanese house, with all the parts, can be erected in two days. They place stones in the ground as post foundations, they then fit the beams in position, fill in the walls and use pegs to fit the shingles in place, making a very swift two-day build of possibly the world's first 'flatpack' house.

The Ad Hoc Ship

The first Englishman in Japan, William Adams, became a samurai, but by trade he was a pilot-navigator and could navigate his way around the globe. He met and became a close retainer to the Shogun Tokugawa Ieyasu. Tokugawa asked him to build him a Western ship, to which Adams said he had no knowledge of shipbuilding, but under his command, Japanese shipbuilders built a Western ship with which the shogun was greatly pleased.

Fire, Fire, Fire

The city of Edo (Tokyo) was a set of disasters waiting to happen ... and they did happen. During the Tokugawa reign between the early 1600s and the mid 1800s there were around fifty major fires in the capital and over a thousand smaller fires. It was in the 1650s that half of the city was destroyed in the Great Fire of Edo, and legend says that it was started by a priest burning a cursed kimono (for more information see the author's work: *The Dark Side of Japan*).

The Dismal Hotel Chain

A *honjin* was an officially established hotel that was sanctioned by the government and passed down a family for generations. These hotels were the places where higher-ranking members of society stayed, and it was custom that they must stay at them. However, because of this custom, the internal aspects were allowed to decline because the guarantee of such clientele meant the management did not have to entice customers. For this reason, lower-quality hotels in old Japan could be nicer than the equivalent to the Ritz, while the equivalent of the Ritz could be worse than a sleazy motel.

The Closed Gates of the City

In the capital of Edo and in Kyoto the cities had very divided districts, with each ward or area cut off by gates, manned by guards, and each little area became a country in its own right with small rulers, councils and populations, where lives could be governed in these micro-worlds. The people, at times, manned their own area and a small watch fire was positioned at each gate and a night-watchman kept an eye on the area. It is said that over 5,000 gates existed in Kyoto, and that if there was a theft or a fight the gates were closed to stop a thief, and that any travellers at night could be identified and movement could be controlled.

The Japanese Michael Angelo

There was an artist/sculptor called Unkei and he is considered to be Japan's equal to Michelangelo. His statues are some of the best the world has to offer, and his religious statues are prized as treasures.

Ticket to Ride

In Japanese cites, with all the nightwatchmen at their gates and traffic at a standstill, only the head of the ward or area could give a special ticket giving permission to leave through the gate by night. This street-chief was responsible for all people inside and knew everyone, and if someone new came to live there they had to have a guarantor.

The Great Hall of 1,000 Mats

Japanese rooms are measured in *tatami* mats; a tea room is four mats and the average modern room can be around ten. It is said that the greatest of lords had halls of 1,000 mats and these were grand buildings that had massive rooms to entertain the very wealthy and privileged.

The Four Types of Japanese Dwelling Place

Japanese buildings fall into four main types:

- The grand structures of the wealthy and powerful
- Town houses which accommodate shops and commerce as well as proprietors
- The houses of the average person including farms
- Religious buildings

Considerations on Buildings

The following are the various matters considered when building in Japan:

Its location in connection with esoteric elements, such as direction, flow of chi, supernatural, etc.

Its alignment with the wind for both hot and cool winds.

Attention to the comfort and accessibility for guests in the planning stage.

The ease of dismantling and moving the building.

Cedar is used by the rich, pine by the poor . (The middle classes use cedar in some areas, such as the entrance, but use pine at the rear of the building.)

Roofs slope towards the front and rear, sloping down over the main entrance and not to the sides.

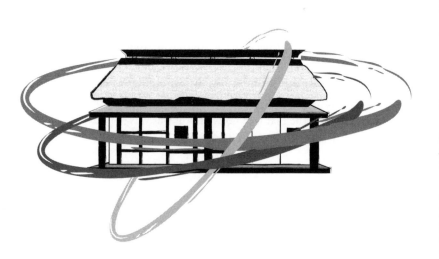

Directions in a Building

No matter which way a building is facing, the following directions are attributed to each side:

The rear of the building is north.
The front of the building is south.
The left is east.
The right is west.

Even if a building is facing north, from the inside the area used as the front is south, and so north becomes south.

The Importance of Seating in a Building

People of importance are seated facing south (the front of a building) with their backs to the north (the rear of the building). After this, the place of importance is on the east, and the west is lower in importance. The lowest position is opposite the highest rank, as they sit with their back to the south (the front) and face north (the rear of the room).

People of wealth would build their buildings as close as possible to this alignment, trying to make the front of the building face south and the rear face north, but if this was not possible, the internals were still considered to be of those directions.

Temple or Shrine?

In Japan nowadays, temples are for Buddhism and shrines are for Shintoism. Any well-seasoned traveller of Japan will point out the differences with glee. But it was not always so; often the two places formed a single entity and even the Japanese could not tell you if it was a shrine or a temple, because often it was both. A temple priest would also be initiated into certain parts of Shinto and many temples – to this day – have small Shinto shrines inside them, one to worship the ways of Buddha, the other to worship the gods. Remember, as history progressed, temples and shrines separated, joined, separated, and joined again.

João Rodigues says that there is no place in the world with carpenters equal to those of Japan. So advanced is their skill that often nails are not used and a complex of interlocking joints are instead made use of. When we imagine old Japan, it is best firstly to imagine wood and straw as predominant over iron and stone.

The Temple in the Hills

The positioning of religious buildings also went through fashions and stages. One fashion was to make the buildings in a very Chinese style, positioned on an open plain and with the correct rituals of *feng shui* attached. However, times changed and later there was a fashion to have remote mountain hideouts which were difficult to access.

The Guardhouse of Hakone

There was one guardhouse in Hakone that was one of the most important guard points in all Japan. It was the divide between the land of the shogun and the land of the emperor and every man, high and low (bar very few), had to stop at this station and show credentials. To try to pass over the mountains nearby was rewarded with the death penalty and crucifixion.

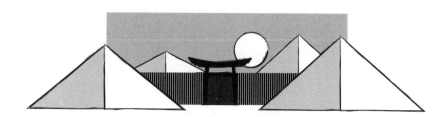

The Importance of Streets in a Town

Streets that ran north–south were primary while those that ran east–west were secondary. The doors of houses should open, if possible, on to a main street, not a secondary one.

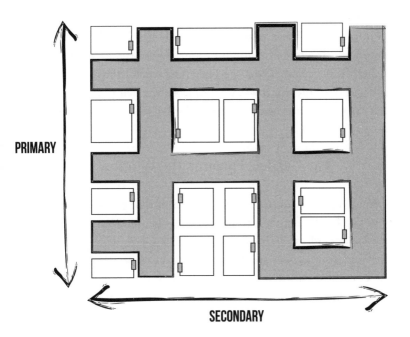

The Grand Gateway

In Japanese culture of old, the grander the gateway, the more prestige a person had. On the whole, the wealthy of Japan would reside in an enclosure. This gives us the image of the classic Japanese tile-roof outer walls which surround a household. In these walls, two gates would normally be fitted, the main gate would be the one through which guests entered and was used in times of importance. These would be extremely grand and expensive gates, and the more luxurious and grandiose the gateway, the richer the occupant. The second gate was one for the servants to use, out of sight, which was used to stock the house with goods, but surprisingly also used to allow the lord to leave with his horse.

The Garden Through the Window

Often, Japanese houses were arranged so that the square exit revealed by sliding doors to the outside would have a miniature garden or landscape framed in the space. Similarly, windows – be they square or round – would have shutters so that, when opened, they revealed nature in miniature. Both of these can be understood as living 'framed paintings' so that the image changed with the seasons.

Art for Each Season

Interior design can reflect the seasons in Japan, and interior art-work should fit with the theme:

Spring – flowers in bloom.
Summer – summer flowers and ripening fruit.
Autumn – ripe fruit and falling leaves.
Winter – leafless trees and winter scenes.

The Stones in the Rain

The diplomat Henry Heusken complained at the state of Japanese roads, saying they were in a sorry state of repair and were no match for the well-paved roads of the West. However, he later discovered that because of the heavy rainfall, the large stones that were causing him a problem were purposely put in place to help prevent soil erosion, even if it hindered traffic.

The Japanese Curtain

The Japanese have sets of cloth they erect around themselves for privacy, just as English people erect windshields on beaches; however, the Japanese version is much more refined and considerably larger. These curtains can be seen in many parts of Japanese life, from war to moon viewing, from suicide to picnics. In Kyoto, people used to go to the countryside to enjoy picnics and surround themselves with such screens, and at times independent parties of people would compose poems and send them to other parties with flowers for their appreciation, a sort of 'send a message to a stranger', while maintaining seclusion and privacy.

Almost Not Kyoto

Everyone is familiar with Japan's cultural capital of Kyoto, founded in the 700s and based on an ideal Chinese system. However, it almost was not the case. The capital in Japan was moved many times: Nara, Kyoto, Kamakura, Edo, etc. However, just before Kyoto, the capital was moved to Nagaoka but this capital only lasted ten years because the court decided to up and move again. The main issue was river flooding, which brought disease, so it was decided to move to a new place, which was Kyoto and was first called Heian. It could have been much different for the average tourist in Japan, and it was only bad irrigation that brought the world the capital of Kyoto instead.

Tokyo and Kyoto

Did you know that '*Kyo*' in Kyoto and Tokyo are the same ideogram and mean capital? Tokyo means the 'eastern capital'.

We Have No Walls to Defend Us

It is often quoted that the men of Sparta were the walls of Sparta and that the city needed none. Well, the same is true for Kyoto, as it also had no defensive walls, the emperor being defended by men and not a castle. That did not stop there being plenty of warfare in Kyoto itself and many bids for political power.

Where the Streets Do Have Names

Many aristocratic names for Japanese families are actually taken from street names in Kyoto where the original families lived, such names being taken from the area their ancestors lived in, showing their connection to the old capital and their closeness to the emperor.

Land Allowance in Kyoto

The following are the legal allowances of land in old Kyoto:

Commoners 450m²
8th rank 3,600m²
5th to 4th rank 7,200m²
3rd rank 14,400m² (a *machi*)

These numbers show the rank system in the Japanese royal court. The amount of land given to the 3rd rank is called '*machi*' and this now means town or city in the Japanese language.

Know Your Place

There was a man in Kyoto who built a house that was bigger than his rank allowed, and used the wrong wood for his status. He had to dismantle the house as punishment.

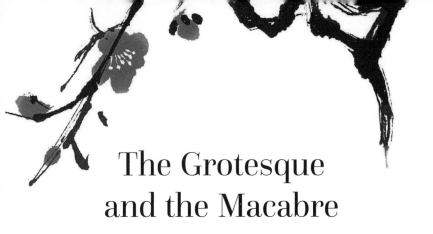

The Grotesque and the Macabre

The Shogun of Terror

The shogun of terror lived in the 1400s and his aim was a Japan controlled by ultimate totalitarianism. He had a personal bodyguard of over 3,000 warriors, all sworn to protect him. He forcefully destroyed others or suppressed them to elevate himself, and he placed unrealistic regulations on court life. In 1441, he was invited to a banquet in his honour and during the meal soldiers stormed the hall, killed him and his courtesans, burnt the place to the ground, took the evil tyrant's head and rode into the night with it on a spike. It was said that not a single warrior committed suicide to follow him into the afterlife and no one really took any form of serious revenge against his murderers. He did some 'good' though; in 1431 there was a famine and the guild of merchants withheld rice to increase the cost for their own profit. He took six guild members and subjected them to trial by boiling water. If they could reach into a boiling cauldron and pick out multiple stones from the bottom, they were then forgiven; if they failed they were killed.

The Princess in the Tower

There was once an evil samurai ruler who wanted another samurai's wife so badly that he had that samurai killed and ordered the wife to be his. The wife said that she needed thirty days to mourn her dead husband and a ceremony in one of the towers to say farewell to him. At the ceremony she leapt out of the tower head first and broke her neck.

The Mad Samurai

Once a samurai who was ill in bed went mad, took up his sword and started to cut down all those around him before he could be stopped. The result was the killing of some of his family members. However, because it was not a crime to kill one's own family, the samurai was not charged.

The Exposed Prostitute

One account describes a woman sold into prostitution who was understandably so unhappy with her lot in life that she tried to run away. When they caught her and brought her back, she was stripped and beaten. They tied her to a pole outside, for all to see, so that any other of the 'house girls' would push the idea of escape from their minds.

Body in the Street

Samurai revenge was very common, and when a samurai killed his victim in revenge he took the head to place on the grave of the person who had previously been murdered. Mitford gives this reality when he says that one morning he woke to find a headless body of a samurai covered with straw near his house after a vendetta undertaken the previous night. He also says that it is a common sight and that revenge was still often performed up to the end of the samurai period.

Lying in Filth

Japanese prisons were hot, cramped and filthy. Often sick men relieved themselves where they were and the rooms became full of human waste. Inmates would kill the sick to stop them fouling everywhere, but these bodies would not be taken away without written permission from above, which did not come quickly. This left rotting corpses and many rats in dark rooms. If the inmates gave the guards any grief, the guards would throw human waste over them from above and reduce or stop the water.

The Dog in the Flames

Mitford had a small house when he first went to Japan, and one night while he was shaving, his Chinese servant came in to him, telling him that a fire had started. Mitford, not knowing the speed at which Japanese town fires spread, said he would be right out. By the time he had finished shaving, his own house was catching fire. In the garden outside, his dog rushed back into the house in a panic, into the flames, and died while taking shelter under a cabinet. Mitford picked up his charred bones the next day. Mitford interestingly says that in Western fires you can hear all the timber crashing and the structure falling, but because Japanese houses are so thin the fire simply consumes them whole.

Dig 'Em Up

In the 1600s, many Christians were martyred. Some people collected their bones as relics. Furthermore, Christian graveyards were emptied and the bones buried elsewhere.

Wake the Dead

Ancient war epics are often laced with old names, lists of heroes, family and clan history, and many other elements that can be considered boring to us. However, from one perspective, giving voice to a name can breathe life into it. So in old Japan, when everyone sat in the dark with a dim light, listening to the bards talk of old deeds, each name that was mentioned was like a beacon in the land of the dead, bringing the long-fallen heroes one step closer to the audience, crossing between worlds.

The Ear-Taker General

There was once a warlord who said that every man, woman and child that did not pay their taxes would have their ears cut off.

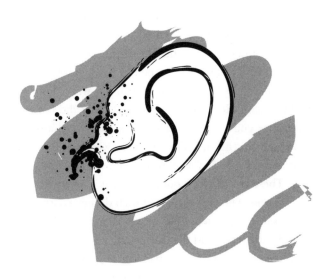

Extreme Torture

Reyer Gysbertsz was in Japan in the 1600s, and his account of the martyrdom of the Japanese Christians is quite sobering. He states that 348 Christians were sent to an area to await their fate. After a time they were brought back and set upon with torture. This included being:

scalded with boiling water
burnt with red-hot irons
beaten with lashes
left naked for days in extreme heat and cold
hung over tubs of snakes
threatened with being roasted alive
threatened with having their children roasted alive.

This led to many believers becoming very ill and, as the point was not to kill them but to show the power of Japan by making them recant, their illnesses were cured by doctors and they were brought back to full health, so that the torture could be repeated. He implies that the women were raped or in some way molested in their treatment but he says that he will not write down what happened to them. He states that some of them did not recant for twenty, forty and even sixty days of torture, but that most of them did recant in the end. Finally, there were about five who would not and their bodies were rotten and stinking, pus-filled, and dying. These last few held out and died as martyrs.

Francois Caron, who also witnessed such things, relates almost exactly the same treatment. He writes that the women were stripped and gang raped and that the people were, in fact, thrown into tubs of vipers. He states that flammable grasses (*hurds*) were placed in women's orifices and then children, fathers, husbands made to light them. Parents had their eyes taken out and were forced to listen to their children being tortured. This account says that most lasted only a few days and recanted, but that a few did last out and die. Others were placed in sheds on beaches and forced to live in them in a constant state of dry and wet. Others were stripped naked and branded on the forehead and then sent away into the forest as outlaws and any person helping them would be killed. Finally, it is said the hardest torture to withstand was being hung upside down in a pit with a small slice on the neck to allow the blood to drain out of the body. With the small dribble of blood coming from the neck, the blood does not swell in the head and kill the person, but leaves them in agony for days on end, and while it was not as gruesome as the others, it was said to be the hardest to withstand. See the film *Silence* for an example of this.

The Dismemberment of Two British Sailors

In 1867, two British sailors from the ship HMS *Icarus* were hacked to death by a mob of samurai during a period of anti-foreign tension.

The Poet Shogun

One shogun, in the age of chivalry, was extremely fond of poetry. It is said that in front of the worship site of the god of war, Hachiman, with gentle snow falling, he was murdered by a deranged nephew who might have been put up to the murder by a powerful female family member manipulating from behind the scenes.

Spellcasters

The famous *yamabushi* went all over Japan performing their rites and using magic. They would take a boy and have the 'devil' invade him to bring forth an oracle or perform other strange rituals. Thousands would gather in holy sites to be ordained through trials and they would wander the country selling their spells.

The First Samurai Martyr

Early on, when Christianity came to Japan, a law was made that only non-military people and those of the lower classes could adopt the faith. However, one samurai, upon hearing the word of God, converted to Christianity. When it was found out, the lord tasked with punishing him, his family, and even the priests themselves, said he should give up the faith and recant later, but he said that once the truth had been found it could not be given up. In the same year that he was baptised, he knelt down, held a cross and prayed to God. His head was then taken off in a single quick blow.

The Killer Monks

One set of monks were warlike, maintaining bows and weapons, and were said to make five new arrows a day. Even though they had strict rules about killing animals, they would go out at night, and rob and murder without a second thought.

Reaching Paradise

There are some eyewitness accounts of people committing suicide to find paradise. One way was to sit on a form of pulpit-chair for days and preach to all would listen. Those who followed them would set out to sea by boat, stones in their clothes. The stones would weigh them down as they threw themselves into the water to reach paradise. Others would bury themselves in a barrel in the ground, calling out the names of the saints until they died.

The Surgeon Under the Knife

There was once a samurai ruler who could not be cured by his surgeon. He asked the doctor why he could not cure him, to which he replied that the ruler was just getting old and no one could stop old age. The ruler had him tied up and chopped into pieces.

Death at the Gates

One festival was so popular that it was deemed an honour to be crushed to death at the gates as they were opened for the festival, so much so that some people purposely went to die there.

Infanticide

Infanticide – the killing of unwanted children – is a worldwide phenomenon, and one record states that in Japan they would stand on the neck of the baby to kill it.

The Boy Thief

There was once a boy who stole from a Western ship. At this, a crew member complained to the street warden, who caught the boy. Within three hours he was sentenced to death. The sailor, horrified, said he did not intend the boy to die, just to be punished. The street warden told him that the wheels of justice had turned and there was no way he could go back on it. If he was to do so it would be his head instead.

The Forms of Execution in Japan

 Beheading

Sawing in half

Roasted alive

Burning

Crucifixion

Torn apart by bulls

Boiled alive

Roasting Alive

There is being burnt alive and there is being roasted alive. Roasting in Japan was to be tied by a chain to a stake and for fires to be set about a person. The victim dashed here and there, but the fire became too hot and they would die thrashing about, anchored to the stake.

Crucify the Lepers

As the persecutions of the Christians started, the command was given that all churches must leave Edo and move to another town and that anyone caught saying mass would be killed. However, there was a hospital which looked after lepers and they continued to conduct mass because they could not move. The authorities heard of this and boarded up the building. However, it appears that there was one non-Christian in the building and it had to be explained to him what had happened. In the morning, soldiers came and said that all Christians must come out and be executed. The Christians came out and were crucified. The man who was there by accident had spent the night learning about the Christian faith, converted and, knowing full well what was going to happen, went out to be executed.

Instant Karma, Medieval Style

An old story tells that when Oda Nobunaga was constructing his grand castle, people both high and low would be involved in the construction. One day he saw a warrior lift the cowl off a woman to see her face, to which he stood up from his tiger skin rug and cut the man's head clean off.

Hell's Gate

The word *gokumon*, 'hell and gate', was used to mean a place or position where the severed heads of criminals were displayed aloft. The bodies of the victims were used for sword practice and test cutting.

The Map of Crucifixion

A samurai official in the 1800s produced maps of Edo for a Mr Von Siebold, but because it was not sanctioned by the authorities, the samurai was crucified and killed. One simply did not give the gift of a map of Edo to a non-Japanese person.

The Assassination of Henry Heusken

The name of Henry Heusken is used often in this book as his account of Japan is outstanding. He was 28 years old, an assistant to Townsend Harris, and a diplomat in Japan. Both of them were tasked by the American government to bring about a treaty between the two great nations. On 15 January 1861, while travelling at night with a small group of men, seven assassins came out of the dark and cut at Henry, who was on horseback. Henry rode away with slashes to each side of his body and was taken back to the government office where he was attended to. He died just after midnight as 16 January arrived. His mother was paid $10,000 (not adjusted) to help support her. His death was one of a few during the dangerous and politically charged times of change in 1800s Japan.

Get it Right or Die

In the time of the Tokugawa shoguns, the *roju*, the great council, would consist of a handful of members who would place proposals for the shogun to review and decide up. If a proposal was declined but at a later date resubmitted, and if it was declined a second time, the councillor submitting it would have to commit suicide. This was recorded by an American diplomat of the time.

To Murder a Wife

In high-ranking households, the women connected to a person of rank would be secluded in the inner sanctum of the house where only young pageboys and maidservants were allowed to enter (in order to prevent infidelity). If a man was seen entering this part of the house, the wife could be put to death.

Iron Maiden? No Way!

One man found his wife talking to another man. As the law prescribed, he had the man commit suicide and he closed the woman up in a casket covered with iron nails on the inside. The Japanese Iron Maiden.

No One Is Safe

João Rodrigues tells us that during the age of wars no one was safe. People dwelt in castles, mountains and the wilderness, but there was seldom safety except for a very few powerful lords, and many dwelt in the shadow of fear. Uncountable atrocities must have taken place beyond the written records that are left behind, families slaughtered and villages sacked, barbaric cruelty now long faded and unrecorded; this period was one of warfare and of cruelty. However, culture and art still continued and it was not total war but a time of continuous wars.

Sword Testing

It is well recorded that the Japanese tested their swords on criminals and corpses, but often it is unknown if the criminal was dead when the sword was tested. However, Romulus Hillsborough tells us that the official executioner for the Tokugawa shogunate, Yamada 'The Beheader' Yuzankaku, did perform test cuts on both dead and live criminals. What is unknown is the number of live subjects that were tested upon.

The Head of the Table

Many Japanese are very trustworthy and value honour above almost everything. However, deception in warfare and conflict was truly acceptable to the samurai. Rodrigues, in his account, tells us that samurai would invite their enemy to a banquet of friendship, an event filled with music, light and laughter, but then halfway through cut off their guests' heads at the very dinner table they were eating at.

Child Suicide

One account states that not only did men and servants commit ritual suicide with loyalty and with a stern face, but that parents wroth with a child would force it to cut open its belly in punishment.

One Dies, You All Die

Some crimes were punishable by forced suicide, but others were punishable by the whole family committing suicide or being killed. In this fashion, there was once a corrupt governor who had taken more tax than was allowed for a prolonged period of time. His entire family was forced to commit suicide. The problem here was that they were samurai, all serving lords, hundreds of miles apart. Riders were sent out to all the different provinces, where all his brothers, sons, uncles and family worked, and upon the eighth day of the eighth month at a prearranged time, they were all forced to commit suicide for a relative many of them might not have even met.

The Blood Temple

Goganji Temple in Oita prefecture in Japan has outer walls of blood red instead of the normal natural brown or limewashed white. In the 1500s, the warrior Kuroda Yoshitaka went to battle with Utsunomiya Shigefusa in that area and the temples were bathed in blood. Utsunomiya died and this temple was built in his honour, but it is said that the blood of the fallen warriors soaked through all attempts to paint them white, and so red paint was used to hide the haunting of their angry ghosts and to disguise the phantom bloodstains.

DEATH POEMS

Before death, in going to war or committing suicide, many Japanese wrote a farewell poem for others to reflect upon.

This tradition is said to have started with Minamoto Yorimasa (1106–80) at the Battle of Uji.

Chop 'Em Up

After a criminal had been executed, it is said that villagers would rush to the body to test their own blades, hacking them to tiny pieces until there was not much left. It should be remembered that until the ban on peasants owning weapons at the end of the 1500s, many people carried swords.

Frankenstein Returns

After an executed criminal had been chopped into small portions, it was sometimes the case that the major parts of the body were stitched back together so that they could chop the body up again, after which they would throw the small parts into a field for animals to eat.

Walls of Terror

Human sacrifice is not a distant thing in Japanese history. When building a wall or a bridge, a volunteer or poor passer-by could end up being a sacrifice to the gods and buried below the foundations. A structure built on the flesh of a human sacrifice was said to be a strong structure.

The Hanging Tree

Two early Christians to be martyred in Japan were hung upside down from a great pine tree. For three days they hung head downwards and many people came to view them. After the three days, they still lived, so they were taken down. One of them was carried, the other walked and they were taken to the execution ground where their heads were cut off.

Heaven, Where Art Thou

It has been said that in early medieval Japan, people would drown themselves, bury themselves alive or find other ways of self-demise so that they could bypass the process of birth and re-birth and go straight to nirvana, the place where the soul ceases to follow this cycle. In old days, such a spectacle might have been not so uncommon, and examples of self-mummification are still exhibited today at certain temples where the bodies of monks who have died in a complex self-mummification process continue to be exhibited.

Next Time, Just Ask

Once a lord was looking for a particular criminal and it was said that a man close by knew of his whereabouts. The man was arrested and threatened, the people in charge saying that if he did not tell them then he would be cruelly tortured by all hell-ish means. To this he replied, 'If you had just asked politely I would have told you what I knew but, as you did not, I shall not say a word.' To this, they tortured him with fire and crushed him between boards and spikes, and yet he died without saying another word.

500 Pieces of Silver for a Christian Priest

Since 1638, the Japanese government had banned Christianity and offered the massive sum of 500 pieces of silver for a hidden priest who was illegally in their lands, preaching the words of the 'heathen' faith. A lesser amount was given for a Japanese Christian, and anyone bearing a letter or communication from a Christian was to be put to death. Again, I recommend you watch the film *Silence* for a good story on this.

Crimes

Crucifixion in Japan involved the criminal tied to a cross – attached with iron manacles – with the legs splayed out, and to have spears thrust through the body. Some chroniclers state that it could take up to eleven thrusts for the person to die, while others say that the first or second spear was aimed at the heart for an instant kill. Crimes that received this punishment were:

- Political crimes
- Patricide
- Matricide
- Servants who had killed a master

The diplomat Henry Heusken tells us that for other crimes they issued beheading, or between 50–100 lashes for lesser crimes. He states that no one could be found guilty until he confessed and, therefore, people who were considered to be guilty were tortured until they confessed.

Haunted Shores

It is said that in olden times, shorelines may have been seen as haunted places, a gap between this world and the next. One theory put forward is that the outcastes of Japan disposed of bodies along rivers (as is done in India) and that these riverbanks and shorelines came to be associated with places of the dead.

Murder on the Highway

A British merchant named Richardson was murdered on the highway in 1862 by samurai from Satsuma, and in response the British bombarded Kagoshima from a warship.

Murder in Kamakura

Major Baldwin and Lieutenant Bird of the British garrison stationed in Yokohama were murdered in 1864 while on an excursion in Kamakura.

The Execution Ground at Shinagawa

In Tokyo today there is a station called Shinagawa. However, a small section of land there for most of the Edo period was the execution ground for over 200 years, and thousands upon thousands of people were executed within its boundaries. Executions were done outside the main hub of the city to stop ghosts attacking, and when parades took place for important visitors, rituals would be performed to spiritually cleanse the area.

To Execute the Dead

If a person to be executed died in jail, the body was placed in an earthen jar and covered with salt. On the day of the execution, the jar was taken to the execution grounds and broken open. The shrivelled body had its joints opened so that it could be crucified. Tied up on the double cross – the arms and legs stretched out – the executioners pierced the sides of the body with spears and 'executed' the criminal.

The Promise of Suicide

When the last shogun resigned from office and the office was eliminated, one of his loyal retainers said that he should now commit ritual suicide, and to show his sincerity he would do it alongside the ex-shogun. The ex-shogun said no thank you; it was a ridiculous idea. The samurai then retired to his quarters and committed suicide.

Songs of Hate

In 1868, a small French river launch was attacked and small band of Frenchmen were injured and some killed, their heads bashed in by poles with metal-hooked tips. This threw diplomacy into chaos and to settle the matter, twenty samurai who were responsible for the action were ordered to commit ritual suicide. This was done in a nearby temple. The first of the twenty men came out, knelt down, and stabbed himself viciously hard. He reached down and pulled out his own entrails and then began to sing songs of hate towards foreign powers and to praise Japan, the land of the gods. His song stopped when he died. It is said that after ten more men had done similar things, the French asked that the executions be stopped.

The Unbelievable Fight

There is an amazing account given by Mitford about 23 March 1868 concerning an assassination attempt by two *ronin*. He was travelling between official events at the height of the anti-foreign sentiment in Japan, with an escort of the British soldiers of the 9th Regiment and 1,500 Japanese soldiers as a guard. However, when the long parade came to a narrow and restricted area, two *ronin*, mad with anger, ambushed them. Unfortunately the vast number of troops could not use their lances and others were stuck a long way back in the parade. The first samurai to engage the *ronin* jumped down from his horse, but his foot became caught in his *hakama* (a form of formal trousers), he stumbled and fell to the ground, just able to parry a blow that was aimed at his head. Another samurai came to his aid and killed the first *ronin* (who was 18 years old), and the warrior who had stumbled hacked off the *ronin*'s head. The second *ronin* (who was 29 years old) tried to kill one of the ministers but only hit

his horse, cutting its nose and slashing its side, and he also lashed out at the British soldiers, wounding a few of them and moving on to Mitford himself. The soldiers shot at the *ronin* and he was wounded somewhat, but carried on. Here Mitford performed an amazing task. He states that there was no point in trying to avoid the Japanese *katana* by stepping back and creating distance, he instead rushed in and wrestled with the man, disarming him. The soldiers of the 9th now seized the *ronin* but he wriggled out of their grasp and ran, to which Mitford states that he gave chase himself and in the end captured the *ronin*. Back at base, they turned the building into a mini hospital because the *ronin* had slashed and cut quite a few soldiers in the flurry. The remaining *ronin* was questioned. It seems he was an ex-monk and had joined the Japanese guards but had been taken up with the idea of killing some Westerners. Mitford gave him tea and tobacco and the *ronin* said that now that he had met a Westerner he regretted his actions and asked for a swift execution. After this, the Japanese questioned him – in a surprisingly friendly way – and found out about three other *ronin* who were waiting further down the street, all of whom were arrested.

After the affair, Mitford lamented that two men could do such damage in such a short space of time and also commented that the British soldiers should no longer use lances as they did not work in the streets of the city. Lastly, he states that Queen Victoria sent British swords of honour to the two samurai who had helped him. If Mitford's words are truly accurate, this episode is an outstanding window into the world of a changing Japan and the excitement and horror of a time of such pressure.

Suicide Instead of Assassination

Throughout this book there are many examples of Japanese hatred towards Western people during the mid 1800s, until the fall of the samurai after 1868. However, it is Mitford who really brings the reality of the dangers home. He states that they were always guarded, day and night, by Japanese and Western guards, they always had a revolver on them, slept with rifles by their beds with the bayonets fixed, lived in compounds for the most part and were advised to shoot anyone on sight who so much as started to draw their sword. He states that in 1867 – one year before the decline of the 'samurai times' and the upcoming revolution – tension was so high that some of the younger diplomats or those accompanying them were so scared of the pressure of assassination that they committed suicide instead. He says one young man went to a back room and fired two shots, the first likely missed because of nerves but the second hit home as the young man shot himself. There were more suicides in the following weeks, making it apparent how dangerous for Westerners this time was. Mitford says that this period of 'knife-edge' stress lasted about four years, before 1868.

The Promise of Tokugawa Ieyasu

One of my favourite examples of samurai 'honour' is the tale of the promise to Toyotomi Hideyoshi by Tokugawa Ieyasu. The leader of all Japan, the mighty warlord Toyotomi Hideyoshi was dying; he made his allied samurai promise to maintain his family power so that his descendants would reign over Japan, and all made the promise to continue his line. After his death, the allied samurai went to war with each other, some siding with the challenger for the 'throne' of Tokugawa and others siding with the 'rightful' Toyotomi clan. Tokugawa defeated them all and then later besieged the Toyotomi Clan at Osaka Castle. Tokugawa offered a form of peace if the Osaka side would fill in the moats of the castle, which they did. He then broke this second promise and slaughtered the whole clan, and then faked his own lineage to make sure he was 'connected' to the correct genealogical line and took the name shogun. The lesson in this tale is that many samurai were loyal to the death, but some (and normally those at the top or those seeking power) were not so loyal. Just be careful when imagining samurai loyalty. At one end of the spectrum, some samurai have outright devotion beyond all things to their own death – like Kusunoki Masashige; at the other, we find broken deathbed promises like that of Tokugawa Ieyasu.

Strange and Curious Things

A Stray Bullet Can Kill

Mitford and Adams – two diplomats in Japan – were taking time to relax after the very dangerous times of the 1868 revolution and restoration of the emperor. Enjoying gardening and the like, the two whiled away the hours with official work. Getting annoyed at a barking dog interfering with the quietness of their surroundings, Adams took out his revolver and shot at it. The bullet ricocheted and hit the cook in the leg. It apparently did little harm and missed the femoral artery, but both Adams and the cook were in deep shock.

The Japanese Flag and the Union Jack

When Prince Arthur (son of Queen Victoria) visited Japan to present the Order of the Garter to the emperor, his ships were met by hordes of people waving the Japanese flag in one hand and the British Union flag in the other, shouting '*Banzai*!' The Japanese even sang 'God Save the King'. At that time, the relationship between Great Britain and Japan was very healthy and the Japanese had just stunned the world by defeating the Russians in battle.

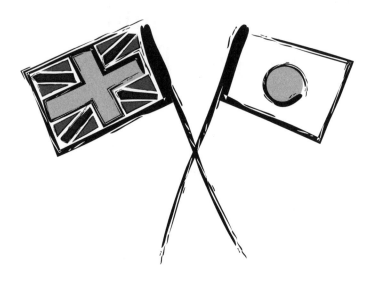

The Human Word

On Prince Arthur's visit to Japan, children swarmed a hillside but, on a single gunshot command, they all took their places and formed the word WELCOME, waved their flags and shouted '*Banzai*!'

The Price of Love

There was once a man who, in the civil wars of the late 1800s, was politically active. He had become the target of a dangerous man, who had put a price on his head. Fleeing from the strife, he met a woman who sheltered him in her home to avoid the assassins. They fell in love and continued to live out their lives in that house. The house had a curious mixture of Japanese style with some newly imported Western luxuries. It appears they actually lived happily ever after.

Difficult Questions

When Catholics first came to Japan they entered into debate with Japan's spiritual leaders and the debates were as striking now as ever. The topics included: creation, why sin is in the world if God is omnipotent, the substance that a soul is made from, the perplexing idea of original sin, how do humans and animals differ in the eyes of God, why did God allow the Devil so much power, and possibly the most difficult one, is God truly unwise to create such a position of unbalance in the affairs of men and to force people into poverty, to create Lucifer, who he knew would fall and Adam, who would sin: they asked how was God so unwise?

Come Here, Come Here!

When the first Westerners came to Japan after the period of isolation, a small but interesting misunderstanding took place. The Japanese thought that the words 'come here, come here' actually meant dog.

The First Labrador in Japan

When Mitford took his pet labrador (which was called Lion) to Japan, the Japanese thought it was a mini bear, or a sheep (which they had only just heard about).

The Lost Trees

In Kamakura – the old samurai capital – is the Great Buddha statue, famous the world over. Originally it had an avenue of trees which ran up the walkway to it. The priest at the time had them cut down so that more crops could be grown in the area.

Predicting Your Future Lover

An old Japanese way of getting a glimpse of your future lover was to turn your nightwear inside out. When sleeping in this manner, you were said to be able to dream of your future partner.

The Albino Horse

In a temple in Kamakura they worshipped albino horses, pure white with pink eyes.

Well Done, Coxswain

When Mitford returned from a sea voyage and had been mistakenly reported as dead in London, he made his way up a river on a small launch boat. An angry anti-foreign mob on a bridge tried to drop a massive stone onto the small craft to sink it. The man at the helm noticed this and sharply turned away, to which Mitford cried out, 'Well done, coxswain!'

The Failed Assassination

Mitford, during his travels in Japan, was at one point bound up in an argument with officials from the district they were in. The two groups argued and debated about the proposed route of the foreign party. After long negotiations and multiple drafts of official letters explaining the change, an agreement was reached and a slightly alternative route was given. When Mitford reached his destination, some of his samurai attendants, who were in a guest house, overheard other samurai talking about how a group of 400 of them had lain in wait for the travelling diplomats but they had not gone on to the road they were supposed to and, thus, the assassination had failed. Mitford heard of this from his samurai and was grateful that the arduous debate had saved his life.

Samurai in Thailand

There is a Japanese village in Thailand. Many exiled Christian samurai and their families created a predominantly Christian village in Buddhist Thailand. The village stands upon a river and in the past was a safe haven from pirates. The village still exists today and can be visited. You can find out more about the village by looking for the Japanese Village Memorial Museum in Ayutthaya, Thailand.

Ancient Japanese Football

Football is said to have come from China, and it even appeared in Japan in the early stages and was known as 'kickball'.

Brandishing British Swords

Once there was a diplomat on his way to talk to the Emperor of Japan but he did not have a large retinue of soldiers to escort him, only two British Army officers on horseback. The two officers rode with their swords drawn and presumably the back of the blades resting on their shoulder as is often the case in military riding. This may not seem like much, but in Japanese society, blades were primarily drawn in public when fighting was to begin. This means that the onlooking samurai and audience were well aware of their readiness to fight if anyone should approach the diplomat, a good use of understanding local customs.

The Monk and the Halberd

Luís Fróis was in the presence of Lord Nobunaga and was in debate with a leading Japanese monk. After a two-hour discussion between the Catholics and the monk, the monk was infused with anger and demanded to be shown a human soul, to which he was told many times that it could not be seen. Afterwards, they entered debate about the body being a prison for the soul and the soul's ascent after death. The monk picked up a *naginata* (a large polearm with a long blade) and made to cut off the head of one of the young Catholics, at which Lord Nobunaga's close retainers seized him. Nobunaga himself said that the behaviour was most unbecoming of a monk and one of the retainers threatened to cut the monk's head off. He was sent out of the room.

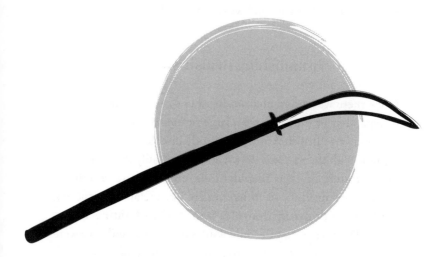

The Death of Tokugawa Ieyasu

Tokugawa Ieyasu is one of, if not the most, famous samurai in Japanese history. The final man of three to unite the country, he died in 1616. Most histories tell us that he died of an illness. However, Mitford – talking 250 years after his death but from Japan – says that Tokugawa died from a war wound that he suffered at the siege of Osaka Castle, and that this wound was the cause of his illness and eventual demise.

Genghis Khan Was a Samurai?

Legend says that the mighty and heroic warrior named Minamoto Yoshitsune (who is similar to Robin Hood and King Arthur for the English) did not die, but in fact left Japan and moved to mainland Asia to become the legendary Genghis Khan, who went on to conquer most of the known world. This, of course, is not true, but it is a legend known in Japan and is discussed in some accounts of Japanese history.

The Last March of the Shogun

The last of the Tokugawa shoguns dismantled his position and office in 1868 and made his way from Kyoto – though normally stationed in Tokyo – to Osaka. He was accompanied by loyal retainers, and Western diplomats saluted him as he rode out of the city as the now ex-shogun, and the line of shoguns came to an end.

The Golden Fish of Water Protection

If you have been to Japan you may have seen massive roof ornaments of golden fish, arching their tails upwards to the sky. These fish are mythical creatures called *shachihoko* – half tiger and half fish – and protect buildings from fire by representing water. In 1873, one of these great fish was sent to Vienna for an exhibition. On the return journey the ship was wrecked, and the fish thought lost in the sea. But the people of the town rallied together and helped save it, putting it back in its rightful place protecting the roof.

The Private Dispute That Built
the Japanese Armed Forces

Two diplomats in Japan in the 1800s were Parkes and Roches, and they hated each other. Roches had offered a deal to train soldiers and modernise the Japanese army. Parkes was so outraged at this move that he brokered a deal to train and modernise the Japanese navy. From this personal rivalry, a first-world military power was established in a very short time.

A Royal Visit

The first royal visitor to meet the Emperor of Japan was the Duke of Edinburgh in 1869. They built him a Western-style house and made a vast amount of preparations. For his arrival, there were a few things that were done which are no longer performed:

Roads that he was to travel were cleaned and repaired and a service was given to the god of the roads.
On the day of his arrival, they held a ceremony at Shinagawa (the execution grounds) to exorcise all the evil spirits from his path.
On his arrival, he was met by a prince of the blood while a ceremony was held to dispel any other evil spirits.

Paper Shutters

At some points in Japanese history, if a person of extreme high rank was passing through a street in a town, the window shutters would have paper put over them so that no one could peep from above into the carriage of the person of prestige. This was done for the Duke of Edinburgh's visit to Japan in the late 1800s.

Revolvers at Midnight

On Mitford's first night in Yokohama, Japan, in the aftermath of a storm, he lodged and slept in a colleague's house. In the evening they talked of the rising hatred towards Westerners and the recent assassinations. In the dead of night, the house began to shake violently, to which the lord drew his revolver and went on the attack. But it was no assassin in the night; it was his first encounter with Japan's frequent and quite violent earthquakes.

Defence of the Home

Once again, Mitford had to defend his home. Late at night he was woken by the breaking of cockleshells – which had been placed about his garden as a warning device – and five or six assailants were coming to murder him. He gave his sword and revolver to his Chinese servant Lin Fu and he took his rifle. They lit the candles and lamps and prepared themselves. The would-be assassins took flight because their target was prepared, and in the morning, when Mitford investigated, he saw marks in the grass where the attackers had slid down a hilly section.

The Italian of the East

One puzzling account from Mitford, British diplomat in Japan, relates that when he arrived in Japan in the 1860s the Japanese studied in the Chinese style and that their language was beautiful and poetic. It was the 'Italian of the East', but after Japan had made tremendous and speedy change in its culture, so too had the language. They no longer had a foundation of classical Chinese, and accompanying the vast speed of change in society came a new wave of vocabulary and ways of speaking. The same way that techno-jargon has entered our language, the techno-jargon of its day entered Japanese and the 'flavour' of the language changed. While at a fundamental level the Japanese remained the same, the aroma and direction of the Japanese language appears to have changed in the late 1800s and early 1900s.

The Japanese Vikings

The Japanese pirates were a little-known group of warriors. An unlikely match in history occurs between the Japanese pirates and the legendary Vikings. The Japanese *wako* and the European Viking were similar in that they were organised into groups of raiders, and they sometimes acted under the authority of a ruler or were independent. They could muster fleets of between 100–200 ships in a raiding party, and they took slaves and engaged in the slave trade. Both moved up rivers to harass local villages and moved further and further inland, becoming a scourge and terror of the seas. In fact, there is an extremely interesting part of Japanese history that is 'missing', and it is that of the samurai mercenaries and pirates in South East Asia. These crews were a menace that terrorised China and Korea, and

Chinese, Korean and Japanese pirates formed conglomerates and became a powerful force to be reckoned with, and were actually only stamped out at a relatively late date. Some bases of operations on the coast of mainland Asia became so 'Japanese' that they could almost have been considered Japanese territory. It is said the native locals actually started to adopt Japanese ways and dress in Japanese fashion. When these pirates were forced to stop, they simply moved their base and raiding parties to a new section of the mainland and continued to operate.

The Transvestite Troops

The idea of mixing male and female clothes was a statement of non-conformity to social norms and became a popular sign of rebellion and a rebellious nature. This style came to be known as *basara* style.

A Game of Stones

From the 1200s to the 1500s saw the rise of a peculiar and often fatal game. Gangs of youths, bandits, and anyone in for a bit of 'fun', would collect stones and have mass fights by launching them at each other. These crowd games became very popular and lasted for a strangely long time in Japanese history and would be a tradition for many generations. It is said that some samurai would get annoyed with being hit by stray stones and rush in, swords slashing, or even join in themselves. What we do know is that these stone-throwing escapades were at times fatal. This 'fun' lasted some time, until the unification of Japan was on the horizon and any anti-conformist attitudes were crushed.

The Dragon of Hakone Lake

Legend says there was once a nine-headed dragon in Hakone Lake that would rise out of the water and take small children and create a terrible ruckus. A holy man came to the aid of the locals, used ancient spells and subdued the dragon, tied it to a tree and cast the tree into the lake, dragging the animal down and chaining the dragon forever. The emperor wished to see this great mage and sent for him, but unfortunately the holy man died on the way and his remains were buried near Hakone. The town nearby holds an annual festival for the dragon.

Potatoes!

We think of Japan as a land of rice; however, it is believed that potatoes were planted by Yoshimune in the 1600s and 1700s, not long after they were planted in England.

The One-Year Change

It is said that before the 1868 revolution, the capital of Edo was a vibrant place, but after the civil war, the end of the shogunate and the decline and almost end of the samurai class, the city had run to disorder, grass grew everywhere, houses dilapidated and palaces in ruins. The once-packed streets alive with ancient tradition and cheer – and of course danger – were now humdrum and pale, waiting to be reborn as modern Tokyo.

The Theft of a Noble Woman

As hostilities broke out before the end of the samurai era, the widow of one of the former shoguns had been kidnapped by clan members from another province. They made their getaway in a ship. In retaliation, those loyal to the shogun's former office burnt down some of their buildings and gave chase in their own ship. Western ships became involved but the whole matter appears to have been sorted with little more affair.

Blind Bards

As with the relating of old tales in the West, bards known as *biwa hoshi* travelled Japan. These song-keepers were blind and played a type of lute called a *biwa* and used guides to travel from place to place. They would set up in each town and play the ancient epics of their culture, spreading the glorious history of old deeds and brave samurai.

The Festival of Hachiman

Hachiman is one of the Japanese gods of war. Before the time of the unification of Japan, on his festival day whole crowds would carry flags and dress in mock armour and carry mock weapons, and the whole assembly would fight. However, things often got out of hand and more lethal weapons were used. Around the time of the unification of Japan and the era of peace, this festival became much more controlled and boys used paper armour and paper flags to fight in the name and for the honour of Hachiman.

THE FESTIVAL OF HACHIMAN

Get Off My Roof!

On the day of the dead, after much ceremony, the Japanese light the way for the dead to return to their world. To make sure no spirit lingers on, they throw stones up on the roof to encourage any unwanted laggers behind to move on to the correct place.

The Scales of Confession

One record tells the story of a high mountain top with a large construction on the top like a set of scales. A person sat on one side of the scales, which would be weighed down in that direction. As the person confessed their sins, the scales would lift up and up, until the sins of the person were gone and they would weigh the same as air and be considered pure.

The Boar

Some gods are connected with animals; some are associated with the boar. One great temple actually kept a boar in a cage in the sacred area in praise of the gods.

The Devil and the Virgin

A strange account tells of a strange ceremony in which a virgin acted like an oracle and communed with a god (the Christians in Japan at the time called it a 'devil'). It is said she had sex with this 'devil' who gave her small fish-scale-like items, then she asked a question and he delivered his answer. Each month, a new virgin was given to the devil.

The Sacred Deer

Many people are aware that, in certain religious sites in Japan, deer walk freely and are considered spiritual animals, and this continues to this day. However, in times of old, to kill one of these deer was to receive a death sentence, property confiscated and the family line discontinued. If a natural death of an animal occurred, the reason for it had to be reported.

The Sacred Fish

In some religious sites in Japan, the ponds were full of fish, and a clap was a signal for feeding to begin. Legend says that anyone capturing and eating a fish would be turned into a leper and any priest or monk eating one would be thrown out of his order.

The Red-Eyed Women of the Sea

There were various families who lived mainly on boats and along the coast. Among them the womenfolk dived deep to catch fish. These woman dived so often for fish that their eyes remained a constant bloodshot red so that you could tell a Japanese diving lady among all others.

The Fire Clock

To know the time in temples, monks would have a wooden container that had flat ash inside of it and they would mark out grooves in the ash in a form of a square. After this they would fill the grooves with a powder that burnt very slowly, but which had been measured with precision. The powder would burn for one Japanese hour, which is around the 120-minute mark. From this, the monks knew what time to ring the bells or perform rites.

The First Elephant in Japan

It was said by Bernardino de Avila Giron that in 1597 an elephant called Don Pedro was given as a gift to Toyotomi Hideyoshi and that it was paraded in the streets of Osaka. So large was the crowd that guards had no effect when trying to beat them back, and some died. Also, he stated, it was not actually the first elephant in Japan and the King of Cambodia had sent one to Japan before, but it had died after a short while.

The Treaty Between America and Japan

Interestingly, the treaty set by Mr Harris in the 1800s between America and Japan was in the three languages of English, Dutch and Japanese. In fact, before this point and around this time, Dutch was much more common than English.

The Reversed Dinner

In 1906, a group of distinguished English nobles visited Japan and one evening had dinner with a mayor. The invitation stated that they should wear Japanese traditional costume. Needing people to help them dress, as they had never done it before, these English nobles and high-ranking persons attended the banquets dressed as a samurai would. However, in contrast, the Japanese guests were all dressed in Western dress, a delightfully strange situation. Both sides were of extremely high social standing, the English dressed as Japanese and the Japanese dressed as English. There is one more element to this. Mitford – who was now a lord – had lived in Japan for many years, he had been there multiple times and, as you will have read in this book, was responsible for much of the transfer and change in Japan, but it seems that this is the first time he had ever worn Japanese clothes. After years of living in Japan, scores of dinners and appointments, he states that he did not know how to wear traditional dress, he found it comfortable, but he did not like the split *tabi* socks. Strange that he, knowing so much about Japan, had only ever worn English clothes there.

Celebrating American Independence in the Time of the Samurai

On 4 July 1857, over a decade before the fall of the samurai, there was a twenty-one-gun salute in Japan, given by the American diplomats there to celebrate independence from Britain, a strange thing indeed.

THE HOT STOMACH STONES

For warmth, the Japanese used to place hot stones in small boxes and wrap them in cloth, this would be put inside the kimono to keep them warm on bitter nights.

Changing Species

In the 1500s the traveller João Rodrigues says that Japan contained animals that could mutate and change shape, and these species-changing animals did this in three ways:

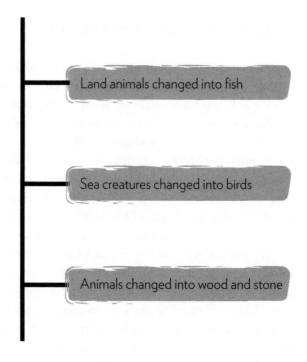

Land animals changed into fish

Sea creatures changed into birds

Animals changed into wood and stone

His account from the early 1600s tells us that fishermen, when they caught a fish, knew that it was once a land animal because of signs within the fish, and also that, at times, creatures that were in mid-change between a land and a sea creature were caught at sea. There were also tales of the wild yam vegetable turning into a snake. The account states that many instances of this occurred in those days.

The Stubborn Mr Townsend Harris

Mr Townsend Harris was a diplomat in Japan in the 1850s, and it appears from the journal of his associate Henry Heusken that Mr Harris could be extremely difficult when dealing with the Japanese. Maybe it was a part of his plan or maybe he was difficult by nature, but he seems to have fixed upon small issues that could have been resolved quietly. For example, in a mountain village on their way to the capital was an ancient checkpoint where all princes and lords had to stop and were subjected to identification and inspection. However, the grand Mr Harris spent two hours insisting that he, not being Japanese, did not need to undergo the cruel and dangerous action of having his face looked at, and so he was allowed to leave the door of his palanquin shut as he passed through. But to his furious horror, his Japanese attendant – who, one assumes, had not been in the two-hour meeting – opened the door as they passed through as he was used to doing, revealing a red-faced Mr Harris, whose honour was in tatters as the party continued onwards. Another example was when visiting the university in Edo, all who went there must pay respects to the statue of Confucius and even the Shogun of Japan must bow before him, to which Mr Harris said, 'not a chance', and declined the visit.

The Complaint of a Pig

The city of Osaka was overrun as the ex-shogun made his escape by American steamer ship. Mitford, fleeing for his life with his men, made his way across frozen banks and paddy fields. After a dangerous day's journey, and with a burning city behind him, he and his troops, hungry and cold, took shelter in a temple. After securing a pig to feed his men, the head monk of the temple refused to let him kill the pig on temple grounds because it is custom that nothing could be killed inside a Japanese temple. To get past this, they had to leave the temple with the pig, take it to an attached vegetable garden and slaughter it there, then return, cook and eat it in the temple.

A Japanese Play About an English Sailor

When Prince Arthur visited Japan in 1906 the Japanese put on a play about the first Englishman in Japan who became a samurai, William Adams. This was done as a show of past friendship between the two countries and as a promotion of Anglo-Japanese relations.

Aim High

In the turmoil of the end of samurai times, a troop of Western soldiers were insulted by the Japanese, to which one of the soldiers took the cover off his lance. Rifle shots and a small skirmish took place and, while only a few people were wounded and the affair ended quickly, it became a problem. Some have said that the Japanese, who were then using Western rifles, were not used to the sights of the gun and shot high, while others say they purposefully were trying to shoot at a foreign flag to discredit the troops. Afterwards it was reported that it was the fault of the Westerners, who had crossed a parade, while others say that this was just an excuse to shift the blame. In the end, the leader of the Japanese force was sentenced to commit suicide. Some people petitioned to save him, but it was decided that he should die or others might find it easy to attack foreign troops.

Japan on the London Money Market

In 1870, the diplomat Mitford was hounded in his London club by people he quite frankly did not know. Perplexed by this sudden interest in him, he investigated and discovered that Japan was about to enter the money markets of London and many moneylenders and men of commerce were after the advice of the Japan-experienced Mitford on the stability of money and society in Japan.

Putting the Flavour Back in Japan

That Woodsmoke Feeling

When a lovely fillet of fish has been hand-smoked, when the smell of spiced wine is in the kitchen or the scent of Christmas is in the air, that is just the way I hope that you are feeling now: not burdened down with names, terms, places and dates, but gently enveloped in a feeling of old Japan. The first Jesuit missionaries said that Japan had become a changed place after Oda Nobunaga revolutionised warfare and state policy. Diplomats who saw the change of Japan brought with the arrival of the West lamented at the loss of Japanese culture to industry. Martial artists and culture enthusiasts who visited Japan during the twentieth-century martial arts boom proudly stated that Japan was no longer the same place, and even I, who did not arrive in Japan until 2004, have now observed the very same thing. The Japan I saw in 2018 is losing its connection to that rich soil below its surface, a soil given to generations of culture and tradition. Posters, adverts and online culture will tell you Japan is a country based on tradition, but even in the short time I have been living in and visiting

Japan, the culture is truly slipping away and such adverts sell 'being Japanese' to the Japanese themselves. A move towards a modern universal world is a grand and beneficial achievement, and it is happening, but it should not be at the expense of cultural identity. The English visit 'English' places to get a feel for old England, to recapture some of that magic that it was to be an English person, but up until the year 2000 it can be said that the Japanese were still Japanese in truth and the generation who actively saw the old world was still alive. There were many things that truly made them uniquely Japanese, from sitting on the floor in their own homes and restaurants, to having those wonderful tables with underneath heat and a quilt to warm the lap area (look up the word *kotatsu*), all the way to their unique view on sex within society and their ardent love of all things Japanese, but also their polite dismissal of things that are not. Now, it can be said that almost all homes in Japan are set up in a Western fashion, with sofas and high dining tables. Their shops and attitudes are taking on a Western feel. The people themselves, while still Japanese, are truly becoming modern and disconnecting from their cultural bedrock, and Japan is fast becoming another modern culture that too quickly is letting go of that which makes it individual. Forward movement is a grand thing, but such forward movement should always maintain some of the things that allowed a country to be identified as itself. There should be universal harmony in the world, national culture and individual identity. The Japanese should rightly join others in a forward-thinking collective manner, but they should also hang on to those small things that maintain their culture, those things that are positive for the nation and give people a sense of collective unity. The Japanese people should stay Japanese.

The Coincidental Routine

In Mitford's journals, he gives the following description of his long but pleasant days in Japan. Upon reading it, it brought warmth into my day as I performed the same routine:

I rise at 7, after a cup of tea in bed – eastern fashion – till 9 I dress and dawdle. Then I have my official letters and work to write, this occupies me till twelve when I breakfast, At 1 I have a class of three Japanese women who I teach English. At about half past 2 I go out, returning at 5, I then work at my translations for about two and a half hours, after which dinner is ready, at 8 I work again until 10 or 11 o'clock when I go to bed.

Mitford's routine

It is with great warmth I would like to describe my days in Japan:

I rise at 8, after a cup of tea or two, I dawdle about. If cold, I light my fire and wait for it to engulf the insides of the stove-burner. After this I sit down to start the first portion of my day's work. I tend not to breakfast until around 12. I move on to the next section of my work, normally translating with one of my team in Japan. I then move on to either my third or fourth project. I then leave my house for a 6-mile walk around the local hills, stopping and saying hello to farmers along the way. After I return, I focus on my letters (emails in this case) and return to study at about 8. In this time I draw the blinds, dim the lights and study some part of ancient Japanese culture and at 11 o'clock I go to bed. With the absence of lighting a fire my routine when in Japan is quite the same.

Cummins' routine

'The old Japan is dead, but its soul
survives in a spirit of patriotism
and chivalry as lofty as any that
the world has seen.'

Mitford

Passing On the Recipe and the Flavour

True artisans need only focus on the intricate details of a subject, as for most people a general and overall idea fulfills in its own right. The aim of this book was to help continue the love of that mysterious country in the East, the Land of the Rising Sun, Japan. While there are ample historical debates, fact-finding missions and theory debunking – with which I myself am involved – there is not enough attention given to the feeling of a culture, there is not enough of a focus on the flavour of something over its base ingredients. Throughout the introduction and this conclusion I have alluded to recipes, cooking and aroma. In this analogy, the ingredients are the base facts of history, the cooking is the debating done by academics, and the flavour is the result of the former two. It should be the flavour that is to be enjoyed by the world, not the debate. The function of historians is to find, as closely as possible, the historical truth of a matter, but they must present their findings to the world in a way that enriches other peoples' lives. Why is history so compelling and why are we, in such a technologically advanced world, obsessed with harking back to another past, and why do we mythologise stories of the future? It is because we as humans need a connection to those who came before us, but also need a direction for the future. We want to know that we have come from somewhere and we are reaching for a destination. It is for this reason that a person will open a book in their lunch hour, on a Sunday afternoon, or on a journey, and will part read, part dream of the future and the past. For this reason, I hope that your 'visit' to Japan has been a pleasant one and that while sat in your chair, or at your desk, or wherever you are located, together our minds have linked across the globe and reached back through time to enjoy past events and that you have connected with the people who actually performed within these stories. It is your imagination that keeps them alive, even though their remains have long decayed in the earth. Lastly, I ask that you pass these stories on, that you tell them to children around a fire or inform a co-worker of something they may not have known and, in this way, we together can keep the rich cultural soil of Japan flowing with memory and keep Japanese culture alive so that these episodes are not lost to the world.

Bibliography

Bodart-Bailey, B., *The Furthest Goal: Engelbert Kaempfer's Encounter with Tokugawa Japan* (Kent: Japan Library, 1995).

Carter, S. D., *Traditional Japanese Poetry: An Anthology* (Stanford: Stanford University Press, 1991).

Cooper, M., *Joao Rodrigues's Account of Sixteenth-Century Japan* (London: Hakluyt Society, 2002).

Cooper, M., *Rodrigues the Interpreter: An Early Jesuit in Japan and China* (Colorado: Weatherhill, 1974).

Cooper, M., *This Island of Japan: Joao Rodrigues' Account of 16th-Century Japan* (Tokyo: Kodansha, 1973).

Cooper, S. J., *They Came to Japan: An Anthology of European Reports on Japan 1543–1640* (Oakland: University of California Press, 1965).

Cortazzi, H., *Mitford's Japan: Recollections, 1866–1906, of Algernon Bertram Mitford, The First Lord Redesdale* (London: Athlone Press, 1985).

Daniels, G., *A Diplomat in Japan* (Oxford: Oxford University Press, 1968).

Elison, G. & B.L. Smith, *Warlords, Artists & Commoners: Japan in the Sixteenth Century* (Honolulu: University of Hawaii Press, 1981).

Gill, R., *Octopussy, Dry Kidney & Blue Spots: Dirty Themes in 18th–19th Century Poetry* (Florida: Paraverse Press, 2007).

Goodman, G. K., *The Dutch Impact on Japan: 1640–1853* (Leiden: Leiden, 1967).

Hall, J., *Japan Before Tokugawa: Political Consolidation and Economic Growth 1500 to 1650* (Princeton: Princeton University Press, 1981).

Hall, J., *The Cambridge History of Japan: Volume 3* (Cambridge: Cambridge University Press, 1990).

Heusken, H., *Japan Journal 1855–1861* (New Jersey: Rutgers University Press, 1964).

Hillsborough, R., *Samurai Tales: Courage, Fidelity and Revenge in the Final Years of the Shogun* (Vermont: Tuttle, 2010).

Passin, H., *Encounter with Japan* (Tokyo: Kodansha, 1982).

Satow, E., *A diplomat in Japan* (Oxford: Oxford University Press, 1968).

Seidensticker, E., *The Gossamer Years: The Diary of a Noblewoman of Heian Japan* (Vermont: Tuttle, 1964).

Souyri, P. F., *The World Turned Upside Down: Medieval Japanese Society* (New York: Columbia University Press, 1998).

Stavros, M., *Kyoto: An Urban History of Japan's Pre-modern Capital* (Honolulu: University of Hawaii Press, 2014).

Totman, C., *Japan Before Perry: A Short History* (Berkeley: University of California, 1981).

Turnbull, S., *Samurai in 100 Objects* (London: Frontline Books, 2016).

Vlastos, S., *Peasant Protests and Uprisings in Tokugawa Japan* (Berkeley: University of California Press, 1986).

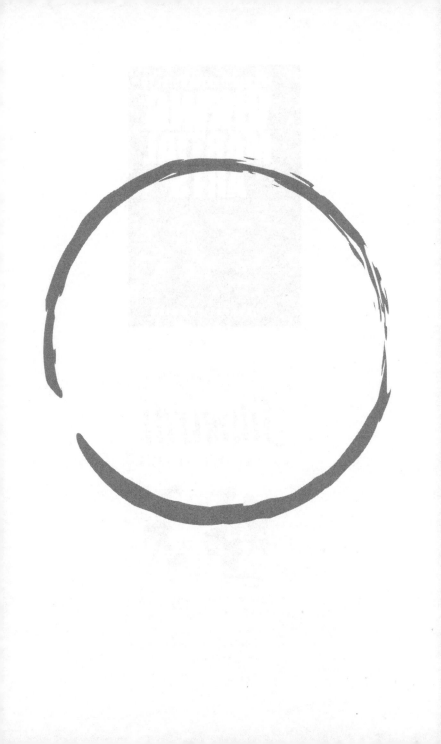

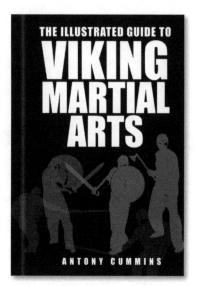

978 0 7509 6745 7

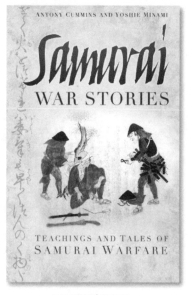

978 0 7524 9000 7

978 0 7524 9210 0

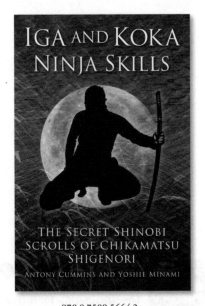

978 0 7509 5664 2

The
History
Press

The destination for history
www.thehistorypress.co.uk